LISTENING TO THE MELODY OF THE MIND

LISTENING TO THE MELODY OF THE MIND

The Psychodynamic Psychotherapist

Rima Brauer and Gerald Faris

JASON ARONSON

Lanham • Boulder • New York • Toronto • Oxford

Published in the United States of America
by Jason Aronson
An imprint of Rowman & Littlefield Publishers, Inc.

A wholly owned subsidiary of
The Rowman & Littlefield Publishing Group, Inc.
4501 Forbes Boulevard, Suite 200, Lanham, Maryland 20706
www.rowmanlittlefield.com

Estover Road
Plymouth PL6 7PY
United Kingdom

British Library Cataloguing in Publication Information Available

Library of Congress Cataloging-in-Publication Data

Brauer, Rima, 1938–
Listening to the melody of the mind : the psychodynamic psychotherapist / Rima Brauer and Gerald Faris.
p. ; cm.
Includes bibliographical references and index.
ISBN-13: 978-0-7657-0613-3 (cloth : alk. paper)
ISBN-10: 0-7657-0613-X (cloth : alk. paper)
ISBN-13: 978-0-7657-0615-7 (electronic)
ISBN-10: 0-7657-0615-6 (electronic)
1. Psychodynamic psychotherapy. I. Faris, Gerald, 1937– II. Title.
[DNLM: 1. Psychotherapy—methods. 2. Memory. 3. Unconscious (Psychology) WM 420 B825l 2009]
RC489.P72B73 2009
616.89'14—dc22 2008027358

Printed in the United States of America

∞™ The paper used in this publication meets the minimum requirements of American National Standard for Information Sciences—Permanence of Paper for Printed Library Materials, ANSI/NISO Z39.48-1992.

For our patients and the melodies
we've heard together

The mind is its own place, and in itself
Can make a heaven of hell, a hell of heaven.

—John Milton, *Paradise Lost*

The nature of being human is that we reprise the condition of childhood either in the imitation or renunciation.

—Rima Brauer, M.D.

The work of the psychodynamic psychotherapist is to engage the invisible dimensions of human thought and feeling.

—Gerald Faris, Ph.D.

This book has been compiled from our experience as psychodynamic psychotherapists. It is a narrative of how we work clinically and therapeutically. Psychodynamic theory is the scaffolding and hidden structure that informs our thinking and practice.

Contents

Preface

THE MELODY OF THE MIND—the harmonies and dissonances emanating from a patient's inner emotional state of affairs, the dark and disruptive, out-of-consciousness, thoughts and feelings; these elements create the distinctiveness of an individual. When helping patients bring greater harmony to their inner worlds, psychodynamic therapists are exposed to those same disruptive, emotional disharmonies and to some of their own. How does a psychotherapist's personal, experiential, and educational history affect the therapeutic outcome? What challenges must a psychotherapy candidate face and surmount to make a good-enough psychodynamic psychotherapist? Not a magical, nor a musical, nor even a brilliant psychotherapist, just a competent and professional one. In short, how do effective psychotherapists listen to those melodies in the minds of their patients?

This book is an attempt to answer these questions and is definitely not a "how-to-do-psychotherapy" book. Such cookbook approaches invite their readers to copy the recipes and come up with something that can be repeated in the same way again and again with predictable results. Psychotherapy, as we understand it is an outgrowth of a two-person relationship. The patient frequently brings some kind of psychological trouble to the therapist who listens with interest and understanding. Out of the talking and educated listening comes a relationship between the two people that enables the patient to ameliorate or resolve the trouble. We believe that this relationship is unique to each patient/therapist pair and cannot be reduced to a formulaic method that demands reproducible and predictable results.

We have had the experience of thousands of psychotherapy sessions and not one of them has ever been the same. We have observed that many therapists have good analytic and reasoning skills but they become anxious when faced with serious psychological trouble. Our book provides insights into one very important attribute of the good therapist: experiential intelligence. We believe that therapists who understand how it develops in all its complexity will be quicker to grasp it, thereby reducing some of the anxiety that comes naturally with this difficult work.

We decided to write a book that would explore the uniqueness of the psychotherapy endeavor from the point of view of the therapeutic relationship as it evolves over time. As we supervised young therapists and acted as sounding boards for more experienced therapists, we became aware of the need for a book concerned with the person of the therapist and his/her feelings. So this book is about the critical, tangible, and intangible characteristics of the effective psychodynamic psychotherapist.

We found a helpful example of the anxiety that can consume a therapist in a recent issue of the *Wall Street Journal* [March 24, 2007]. It dealt with a lawsuit brought against Allegheny College in Meadville, Pennsylvania, and a school counselor—Ms. Kondrot—and Dr. Richards, a psychiatrist. The parents of a young man, Mr. Mahoney, sued for damages related to their son's suicide by a drug overdose. At that time, the boy's counselor was not licensed in the state of Pennsylvania. She had consulted with professional people whom she thought could be helpful. Shortly before the suicide she had asked Mr. Mahoney if he had pills. He replied that he would not overdose. Ms. Kondrot had followed the counseling script of inquiring about any inclinations he might have had to overdose. But Mr. Mahoney left that afternoon and hung himself with his dog's leash.[1]

Reading about the trial and the story of the dog's leash, one can experience a sinking feeling. It was reported that Ms. Kondrot, at one point "started to cry and told Mr. Mahoney she felt he needed more help than she could provide."[2] We believe that the counselor was flooded with anxiety and feelings of helplessness, and as she expressed this deep despair, she unknowingly communicated to Mr. Mahoney that he couldn't be helped at all. His depression then triumphed over their relationship and over his life.

So our intent is to provide a comprehensive exploration of the person who is the therapist. The key issue of experiential intelligence organizes our thinking. By *experiential intelligence* we mean the accumulated emotional and psychological awareness and knowledge of nuance and subtlety present in the two-person therapy hour. It helps the therapist to take the measure of a patient's emotional temperature and vulnerability to extreme actions. The therapist should feel comfortable with Harry Stack Sullivan's aphorism, "We are all more simply human than otherwise."[3] We intend to discuss how this one very critical attribute of the psychodynamic therapist, who works within the two-person psychotherapy paradigm, affects the treatment of patients across a broad spectrum of psychological disturbances.

As far as we can determine, there are many books about the practice of psychotherapy. But none offers an enhanced descriptive account of the elements that comprise experiential intelligence.

Psychotherapy has been described humorously as the art of practicing a science that doesn't exist. We believe that the practice of psychodynamic psychotherapy draws on both art and science, a reality verified by a close read of the scholarly journals that stand alongside classical Greek drama. Psychotherapy should be conducted only by those properly trained and steeped in the empirically based literature. Insightful and well-trained therapists should, therefore, draw heavily from the scientific disciplines of child development, medical science, biology, neuroscience, psychology, and sociology. To tap into the great body of research in such areas of study means the well-read therapist must be able to assimilate the contributions from a rather broad array of specialties. That is a daunting task and is not for the intellectually faint of heart.

A competent psychodynamic psychotherapist must come to understand the invisible and complex unconscious elements of motivation that lie beneath the patient's inner conflicts. Poets have noted self-defeating, destructive, and perverse human behaviors almost from the beginning of human history. The irrational impulse was one of the two great narratives in Greek antiquity (the other the logical), culminating in the insightful plays of the great tragedians. As the eminent physicist Max Born commented in reflecting on the world's misery during the early twentieth century, "the world is not ruled by reason . . . even less by love."[4] Man's motivations are complex. Psychology is the field of study that looks into man's inner life. The therapist guides that endeavor.

Most clinicians will tell you that the patients they treat in psychotherapy are hoping to resolve inner conflicts that interfere with their lives. Patients frequently know they have to examine their backgrounds or perhaps biologically inherited disorders. Cultural humor about what patients expect to the contrary, they do not generally anticipate any efforts to blame their parents. In fact most patients actively resist doing so. But it is perhaps a commonplace in modern times that we all speak of coming to know our darker sides in terms of our hidden motives. The enduring truths about the unconscious aspect of the human condition were understood by the poets long before Freud who started the "talking cure." As Freud once pointed out, "The poets and philosophers before me discovered the unconscious."[5] It is no surprise to learn that Freud read the Greek playwrights' tragedies of the fourth and fifth centuries.

Psychoanalytic ideas in clinical work seem to capture our intuitive sense of the need to look more deeply at ourselves, just as Shakespeare still intrigues us because his masterpieces explore the depths of human fantasy and feeling. In this book we offer our perspectives to the psychodynamic psychotherapists in training and newly practicing psychotherapists who are readying themselves to cultivate a capacity for tuning in to the disharmonious melodies they will soon be hearing. The goal is to help them develop and use their experiential intelligence in the powerful and demanding work of a two-person psychotherapy. We imagine our findings will be of value to veteran psychotherapists and to many patients as well.

Finally, the title of the book *Listening to the Melody of the Mind* reflects our view of a parallel between music and the psychology of mental life. It has been said that music bypasses one's thinking and goes straight to one's feelings. Redundancy in speech, repetition in language, vocal qualities such as tone and pitch as well as non-verbal, gestural communication, for example, form the basis of a personal rhythm that we liken to the melody of the mind. We hope that our use of melody-as-metaphor can help clarify the complex nature of the mind and its processes—the ultimate focal point of the psychotherapist. A melody organizes the basic elements of music into a synthesized and unified symphony, thereby creating rich, subtle, and complex feelings. Similarly, a mind tends to organize the full range of our experiences, thoughts, and feelings into a synthesized whole and create a rich melody of the self in the interior as well as in the world.

Notes

1. Elizabeth Bernstein, "After a Suicide, Privacy on Trial," *Wall Street Journal* (March 24, 2007).
2. Bernstein, "After a Suicide."
3. Harry Stack Sullivan, *Clinical Studies in Psychiatry* (New York: Norton, 1973), 26.
4. Werner Heisenberg, "Letter to Einstein," in *Born-Einstein Letters* (New York: MacMillan, 2005).
5. Lionel Trilling, "Freud and Literature," in *The Liberal Imagination* (New York: Doubleday, 1953), 32.

Acknowledgments

We wish to thank all those who supported, in word or deed, the writing of our work. We are especially grateful to Lee Brauer, MD; Ralph Faris, PhD; Graham Gibbard, PhD; Michael Fulco, PhD; and Theodore Mucha, MD.

We are, of course, completely responsible for any errors that might appear in this book.

I

INTRODUCTION

1

Two Minds Establish a Psychotherapy

The disharmonious melodies of life reside in the unconscious mind.

WE ARE PSYCHOTHERAPISTS WHO BELIEVE that unconscious processes are part of the human mind and that the mind is much more than the brain, the self, and interactions with the immediate environment. The mind has a uniqueness as well as a structural organization. The mind is concerned with thoughts, feelings, and behaviors. As therapists we are engaged in helping patients through the process of exploring their own minds. When we talk about a psychodynamic psychotherapist, we are referring to a therapist who practices a form of psychotherapy that is "insight-oriented" and "exploratory," not cognitive or behavioral.

We are not speaking of counseling or of case management. Counseling is about emotional support, advising, and educating. Case management is a process whereby the needs of the patient and perhaps the family are assessed by an appropriate professional who follows the situation and coordinates, evaluates, and advocates for various services. Each of these disciplines is an important helping profession. The distinctions among these disciplines may be hard for non-professional people to make.

Characteristics of patience, attentiveness, and an alertness to the unconscious will form part of the contribution of the therapist in the two-person psychotherapy relationship. The relationship must be constructed to frame the problem and prevent the patient from acting precipitously. How will the relationship allow both patient and therapist to tolerate and examine uncomfortable feelings that underlie thoughts and behaviors that characterize the patient's psychological trouble? The therapist is knowledgeable about uncomfortable feelings and develops a safe haven in the room so that when he says to the patient, "let's consider these uncomfortable feelings," the patient listens. The therapist listens so that the patient is able to imagine new thoughts and contemplate new ideas and feelings about his inner world. This novel creation around psychological issues within the two-party relationship is the foundation of a good psychotherapy. The structure of boundaries, point of view, and special type of listening provide a holding environment for both patient and therapist in the same room.

Although psychodynamic psychotherapy can include the actions of counseling and occasionally some of the actions of case management, psychodynamic psychotherapy is different, and more complicated. This book is about just how different and how complex. We believe the practice of psychodynamic therapy is a profound challenge to the intellect and the personality of the therapist.

The work of the psychotherapist is to accompany the patient on a journey. The journey is in the form of a search to understand the meaning of the dissonant symphony of thoughts and feelings, symptoms and behaviors that plague his life, and to help the patient toward greater emotional resolution of his underlying conflicts. The hoped-for outcome involves a better perspective on one's life and circumstance. For the purposes of this book, the terms "psychotherapist" and "psychodynamic psychotherapist" refer to our specific mental health professional person regardless of his educational credentials. Although we are concerned with psychodynamic psychotherapy, we believe that most empirically based psychotherapies such as cognitive and behavioral therapies could be attuned to most of the issues discussed here as well.

The distinction between mind and brain is important for clinical efficacy. The brain forms the biologic substrate of the mind. The clinical work we cite in support of our understanding of psychotherapy evolves from the point of view that the mind is a complex development from birth onward encompassing psychosocial, educational, and biologic factors. Much of what we know about the mind comes from clinical case studies. We do not know precisely what happened to us when we were young, but we may have limited access to the past through our senses, our attachments, and our memories that form a naturalistic narrative in forming the clinical case study.

We use empirical findings in hopes of recognizing scientific truths. We use naturalistic observations in hopes of accompanying the patient on a search for personal or psychological truth. Empirical findings may relate to the brain as well as to how the brain and mind may interact. Clinical findings, on the other hand, refer to the mind and how the patient's environment and personal history influence the mind. The disciplines of hard science, biology, and chemistry are used to study how medical science, molecular biology, neurology, and genetics relate to the brain. Clinical psychology is a softer science where the evidence may be indirect and is concerned with mind. Other divisions of psychology such as cognitive science, neuroscience, and experimental psychology bridge the space between mind and brain.

The psychodynamic therapist uses a conceptual model of a mind that has both conscious and unconscious elements. The therapist uses the concept of subconscious or preconscious to have a way of talking with the patient about things that are just under the surface of awareness. With tact and skill the clinician may be able to bring memories, thoughts, and feelings to the surface. The presumption that increased self-knowledge will allow the clinical work to progress is a critical part of the paradigm.

Feelings may be powerful determinants of *thoughts* and *behaviors* and will be the bedrock of the clinician's ability to listen to the melody of the mind. They help form the interactive joint endeavor between patient and therapist and will help authenticate the clinical relationship by providing the interest for both patient and therapist to continue on a therapeutic journey together. They form the attachment linkages from one memory to another as reality intervenes in separate ways for patient and therapist.

Feelings can be attuned in range from intense to mild or neutral, from negative to positive. They range from conscious to slightly unconscious to completely unconscious and from visible to invisible, from covert to overt. We consider these feelings and thoughts to be real life continuums that constitute the melodies of the mind. These melodies can be repetitious themes, they can be discordant but functional harmonies, and they can have many disguised variations of the same emotional score. Attempts to confine human experience and motivations to more narrowly defined, superficial melodies and to employ easy remedies underestimate the depth of human mental life. Examining overt signs and symptoms with a "what you see is all there is" attitude is of limited clinical value.

Feelings are complicated human experiences and can be used as defenses against other emotions. When a patient talks about being bored, he is often trying to disguise to himself a more painful emotion such as anger or envy. Distortions can minimize or maximize common feelings. Feelings can be displaced. They can be avoided and they can be converted. For example, depression can be converted into anger; anxiety can be converted into control; loneliness can be converted into attention getting. It is a considerable challenge for a therapist to translate clinical concepts such as these from books to the patient.

How is the experiential intelligence of a psychotherapist manifested? How does the experiential intelligence develop out of the special two-person therapy? The motivation of the therapist involves a curiosity and interest to know the mysteries of the mind. The therapist pays attention to small meaningful clues that might lie out of the awareness of the patient. In some ways, therapists are similar to artists in that they may experience a beach or a landscape differently from a casual observer.

Examples of therapeutic artistry and experiential intelligence can be found in the cases briefly cited in several sections of this book. They can be detected in the observations of many of history's great therapists—consider Harry Stack Sullivan's (1947) insightful and clinically useful concept of an "*empathic linkage*" between mother and infant, a concept that makes the idea of child development more meaningful.[1] How helpful for the therapist to be aware of the effect a mother's psychological attunement has on a child's emotional well-being and capacities as an adult.

Or consider aphorisms offered to therapists by Semrad (1980):

> We don't think often, how useful it can be for somebody to be able to go where he can get mad as hell—and nothing happens. People are willing to pay a lot of money for that.
>
> One of the main functions of anger is it allows one to say what he really thinks. He may take it back later when he cools down, but it's important to remember what he said and to deal with it, because that's where the heart of the feeling is.
>
> One of the hardest things for people to get used to is to allow people to come and go in their life, and to do the necessary affective work, namely, taking their investment from what they had before, putting it back in themselves, and then reinvesting it into something or someone else. This is the hardest work that goes into the whole phenomenon of growth and development. Growth in terms of self-differentiation and self-maturation is a very sad process.
>
> Weaning is a very sad experience for everybody, whether it's weaning from the breast itself, or whether it's weaning from some substitute of the breast. The first loss is giving up something that one has had, and it becomes the prototype of all later mourning experience. It's very sad to allow yourself to remember something that has been—that is no more.[2]

We need cognition, reflection, and emotion to practice the fine art of psychotherapy. We need the ability to think productively and strategically based on scientific principles. We need to have the capacity to reflect on our cognitive understanding and our emotional reactions. We need emotional capacity and understanding of ourselves and our patients and the willingness to put the emotions in a special place between cognition and reflection. In that special place we can listen to and follow the musical rhythms that inform our psychotherapy endeavor.

The psychotherapist is an ordinary human being who processes data by using imagination in a unique internal way and by using reasoning in a valid external way. Imagination tends to be broad, impressionistic, and emotional;

imagination may use symbols, displacements, and condensation; imagination makes jokes, slips, and errors and forgets. On the other hand, reasoning relies on thinking, logic, specificity, and exactness. Imagination favors human connections and romantic fantasies. Reasoning favors separateness and individuality. We think that in the kind of two-person relationship of psychodynamic therapy, the art of it lives in the realm of imagination and the science of it lives in the realm of reasoning.

A psychodynamic psychotherapist lives in the space between the realm of imagination and the realm of reasoning. The competent psychotherapist may feel attached and separate at the same time and with the same patient. This apparent contradiction is nevertheless a clinical truth. Such a psychotherapist is able to quickly move from the imagination to the real and back again while feeling emotional resonances and thinking organized clinical thoughts. The individuality and humanity of each psychotherapist brings to the clinical situation a unique style of back and forth in the intermediate space between internal and external reality. Admittedly abstract and hard to concretize, these ideas do capture what we believe to be the *sine qua non* of the psychodynamic psychotherapist in the act of listening to the melody of the mind.

Consistent with the above paradigm, we consider that well-trained psychodynamic psychotherapists are most likely to understand the following:

1. As we indicated, human actions are divided into three categories—*thoughts*, *behaviors*, and *feelings*. These three categories generally interact and affect each other like a more or less integrated musical composition. Each category has a range or continuum of application. For example, thoughts and beliefs can be as smoothly synchronous as a Rachmaninoff concerto, or as discordant and cacophonous as an orchestra with each member tuning his own instrument in preparation for the concert. Behaviors can be as controlled and contained as a Schumann symphony or as exuberant as Tchaikovsky's "1812 Overture." In another dimension, behaviors can be very aggressive, moderately aggressive, or rather passive, avoidant, and non-assertive.
2. That the most baffling, complex, and controlling aspects of human actions are found in the melodies of mind. We note therefore, that a competent psychodynamic psychotherapist requires solid training and expertise in the many complex/sophisticated concepts relating to mental processes. To be of help to the wide variety of patients beset by emotional conflicts, the therapist needs to have a suitable temperament and personality.
3. That behaviors may be relatively easy to modify, thoughts and beliefs may be modifiable but less easily than behaviors. Feelings are exceptionally

> difficult to modify. There are important symptoms beyond the more well-known ones of anxiety, depression, guilt, and shame. For example, a patient seeks treatment because he is tortured by self-punitive, morbid thoughts or because of suicidal and homicidal urges. Another may be struggling with feelings of jealousy to the point of paranoia. A person may use (unconsciously) religious fervor to the exclusion of reasonable perspectives as a way of controlling some ominous melody of mind he cannot stop from playing. Symptomatic behaviors appear in many forms as in phobias and rituals or perversions and addictions. Any typical personality style can be deformed into a knot of bodily symptoms.

We believe that the talking cure works by listening to the melody of the mind and allowing the mind to be moved to a better place. The idea that many of our thoughts and feelings are not conscious is still surprising to many, but neuro-scientific research is putting in pictures what clinicians of the talking cure have previously put in words.

The concept that invisible, unconscious processes are always present like the hidden sixth-sevenths of an iceberg is a core belief of a psychodynamic therapist. From our point of view, no matter what the form of psychotherapy, these unconscious processes are the predominant influence on all human behavior.

Applying our musical metaphor we would say that melodies from the unconscious mind be may be experienced by a listening therapist as soft, subtle, and barely heard on the one hand and escalate all the way to loud, brassy, and glass shattering on the other. Sometimes humans are completely unaware of the subtle harmonies of another's unconscious feelings while at other times, we sense their presence. Even the loud, brassy patterns of behavior can mask some of the hidden melodies of mental life, such as a quietly mournful or an agitated, anxious inner refrain.

We further believe that developmental history is critically important in understanding adult behavior. Many clinicians today agree with William Wadsworth's often quoted "the child is father of the man." Within the limits set by constitutional factors, the vicissitudes of childhood and adolescence are the critical determinants of what a person will be like as an adult. The melody of mind is strongly influenced by the melodies internalized from the childhood environment.

Another core principle of our psychotherapy endeavor relies on understanding conflict. With internal conflict, we struggle with ourselves as much as we do with the external world. The comment that fits, from the comic strip Pogo we think, is "we have met the enemy and he is us." We consider that all human beings, to varying degrees, struggle with the conflict between needs and desires, on the one hand, and anxiety and despair on the other.

These three ideas—unconscious processes, developmental history, and internal conflicts—reflect what we believe are the crucial concepts in the mind of the competent psychodynamic psychotherapist. *The real demons of life reside in the unconscious mind, and the melodies they play are striking and compelling if the therapist can hear them.*

Today we recognize the value of these three ideas. Every therapist has seen a couple where a wife was responding to a partner as if he were her father, or vice versa, that is, the husband responds to the wife as if she were his mother. Unconsciously responding in this way not only causes a loss of perspective about the spouse, but also tends to make the husband feel more like a child—a state of feeling more typical when one is talking with one's parent.

This wife might complain about her husband because he wasn't as available as she needed him to be. She might also complain that her daughter didn't come home for a holiday. She might complain that her mother-in-law is a poor cook and that something isn't going right at her office. Such complaints seem to touch every aspect of her emotional sense of being and resonate like a background melody in the therapist's mind.

The wife in therapy might recall how she felt "as a child" with her father, and recognize the return of those feelings with her partner. She might then be able, eventually, to stop and recognize that the feelings and behaviors were more suited to the past memory, and not to the present circumstances, an old melody rather than a new one.

We all have similar experiences throughout our lifetimes. Such experiences may also be melodious, pleasant, and adaptive. For example, a woman remembers that her father bought her a typewriter, her first one. She now remembers him lovingly when she buys her children their first computers. But the complaining wife didn't have such a nice father. He screamed and swore at her so much that she could barely do her schoolwork.

Anxiety is a feeling that causes stress, or is it the other way around? What may be stressful for one person may not be stressful for another. A person who cuts himself may be soothed by blood-letting, while a person who runs for the nearest box of Band-Aids when he is peeling potatoes and scrapes himself feels anxious at the sight of blood. Of course the average person is somewhere in between feeling "that's just a little blood" and "I'll be really frantic if I'm in a car accident and there's a lot of blood."

Developmentally, an infant of six weeks has some consciousness through smells and memory, although thinking in the adult mode remains to be developed over time. The current view is that if visual perception, significant aspects of memory, or difficulties in physical movements are affected by unconscious forces, then serious psychological problems probably are present.

If a therapist is trained superficially, he may believe that if he just exposes the patient's hidden, unconscious feelings and ideas, the patient will get better. Oh, but the patient will resist such knowledge. When it might pertain to ourselves, such knowledge makes us anxious, and we resist first by denial, then by avoidance, sometimes by rationalization and sublimation.

Clinicians and researchers have been working for the past hundred years to clarify the essence of and refine the variety of techniques and concepts that currently are employed in what one of Freud's patients called "the talking cure."[3] So we must be humble and diligent in our appreciation of the human brain with its billions of neurons plus many more billions of synaptic connections. The brain functions to promote the development of an incredibly complex human mind with a seemingly endless capacity for creativity and irrationality. Psychoanalytic thinkers have long respected the pervasive influence of unconscious mentation. Jonathan Lear, in a series of lectures at Harvard, *Happiness, Death, and the Remainder of Life* (2002) in the Tanner Lectures of Human Values, proposes that the mind actually disrupts itself as a means of remaining active and creative. Philosophers, sociologists, psychologists, anthropologists, and biologists look in wonder and confusion at the richness, creativity, and irrationality they find in human behavior.[4]

Any psychotherapist who only pays lip service to this complexity is in danger of confounding the therapy and is doing a disservice to the patient. It is our hope that by understanding the requirements, challenges, and limitations found in this work, we will be able to give an accurate description of what it takes to listen to the melody of the mind.

Notes

1. Helen Swick, Mary Ladd Gawel, and Marry Perry Gobbon, Eds., *The Collected Works of Harry Stack Sullivan*, vol. 1, (New York: Norton, 1964), 257.
2. Elvin V. Semrad, *Semrad: The Heart of a Therapist*, ed. Susan Rako and Harvey Mazer (New York: Jason Aronson, 1984), 101–27.
3. Sigmund Freud and Josef Breuer, *Studies in Hysteria*, The Penguin Freud Library, vol. 3 (New York: Penguin Books, 1991), 83.
4. Jonathan Lear, *Open Minded: Working Out the Logic of the Soul* (Boston: Harvard University Press, 1998), 84.

2

How the Talking Cure Works

What does it mean?

WHEN WE FEEL ANXIOUS WITHIN OURSELVES or in reference to an external situation, we usually have the coping skills to adapt to the in*tra*personal situation, that is, I don't want to go on vacation alone so I'll go with a friend, a family member, or group. If we're afraid to go to Africa because we might develop a strange illness, we might choose to go to a medically safer place. But if we have chosen to go to a safe vacation place with a good friend and find ourselves fighting with the friend and regretting that we came, then we have advanced to the level of interpersonal conflict. We might blame a friend for being inconsiderate, cheap, or rigid depending on the situation. By the time we're back home we might begin to wonder whether or not we might have contributed to the difficulty. We realize that some of us have no tolerance for psychological thinking or psychological mindedness and may prefer to see things as black or white, or maybe "what you see is all there is."

If we notice a pattern of fighting and regretting that repeats itself in various ways in different circumstances such as at work, school, or with our love relationships, we might consider talking things over with a family member, a friend, a religious person, a teacher, or a neighbor. If our social attempts to solve the problem don't seem to be helpful, we turn to self-help books, magazine articles, and educational guides. We usually keep on trying to improve our situation and our relationships. When we don't succeed we might try to talk with a professional talking person.

The emotional relief we feel initially when we consult a professional talking person is often dramatic regardless of what the person says. The professional talking person listens, advises, and cares about our difficulties. It's as if we run home to mother when we've had a bad fall. We feel relieved when she's there, puts her arms around us, and says reassuring things. When we feel better, we go back outside and try to ride the bicycle again. When we believe the professional listener/reassurer, we feel capable of going back into the world, picking ourselves up, and trying again.

Technically, this emotional relief is a common first manifestation of positive transference. This small initial transference enables both the professional listener and patient/client to make a second appointment. Most people have fewer than ten appointments. After some emotional relief and reassurance most of us can resume our lives with a bit of encouragement and education. Most of us have common sense, moderate education, friends and family. We have ordinary skills that allow us to make new friends and adapt to new situations. Some of us, however, get stuck with old melodies, that is, behavior patterns from old situations. Some of us project a personal myth onto the screen of life with unfortunate consequences.

When we get stuck, we may want to find a way out of the quagmire but don't know how. If we believe that a therapist will help us find a new direction for our difficult life situation, we'll likely trust that person to be helpful. Initially, the patient brings positive feelings and expectations, and the therapist listens, cares, and tries to say helpful things. If the talking goes well in the ordinary sense, the patient will feel better and the therapist will be gratified. Treatment will be relatively short and everyone, including the insurance company, will have had a rewarding experience.

Sometimes the same unconscious feelings or ideas that stood in the patient's way when he went on vacation with his best friend will come to the therapy situation also, presenting a significant challenge to the patient–therapist interaction. That's when the treatment gets hard for the patient and the therapist. It will be the goal of the therapy to point out the repetition and re-creation of these obstacles in the treatment situation. If the therapist is skillful, smart, and tactful enough to do this, the treatment will continue.

Often our emotions have not educated us as well as we would like. Our reasoning and problem solving skills may not be up to the job of reworking emotional conflicts. The more powerful the feeling the more likely those feelings will be interpreted as facts. Feelings of guilt will force the person to believe he is guilty. Feelings of anger will force the person to believe the other is guilty. None of these powerful feelings will convey or permit dispassionate thinking. Talking with a calm, interested observer breaks the distortion bridge between fact and feeling.

So maybe we try a vacation, a new boyfriend, a new job, or an old activity, but an attempt to change the external situation will work only if the external situation is *in fact* the emotional problem. Stress in the workplace or conflicts between spouses, parents and children, or family members will generate emotional problems at times. When work is fine, the new boyfriend is great, the vacation was perfect and we still have emotional nightmares, it might appear to us that the emotional problem is *within.*

The psychodynamic psychotherapist is an explorer on a journey with the patient to gather material about the patient and come to an understanding about its meaning. The patient usually will have small but accumulating emotional reactions as the meaning of the material becomes clearer. Sometimes, there will be a larger, "aha" moment. The patient's dawning awareness of the meaning of his/her behaviors, perceptions, and symptoms is a source of the relief experienced. We humans like to know what makes us tick, especially if the ticking is causing us trouble. We want to hear our own melody of mind. And then we might want to orchestrate it, too. If we can, then we would have another source of relief as well. If we cannot, we might have some conflicts and then a deepening of the psychotherapy experience might be of further help.

3

When the Therapist Is Good Enough

A psychodynamic psychotherapist must see the person in the disguise of patient.

THE PSYCHODYNAMIC PSYCHOTHERAPIST TRIES TO GRASP THE NATURE of the person in the disguise of a patient. We submit that this work of attuning to a patient's unconscious emotional discord should be informed by an experiential intelligence, that is, knowledge blended with intuition, broadly derived from empirically based psychological frameworks, in-depth self-awareness, and clinical experience. Experiential intelligence, simply stated, helps the therapist to do a good job.

We are also suggesting that the practice of psychotherapy today is greatly complicated by dual and conflicting challenges for the psychodynamic psychotherapist. There have been broad, impressive advances in theory and empirical findings that inform and deepen our understanding of the processes underlying psychotherapy. In the past forty years, the results of countless numbers of well constructed research efforts and studies have dramatically transformed the technique and practice of psychotherapy.

Research in infant and child development has clarified and enhanced our grasp of cognitive and emotional processes. Brain imaging techniques have begun to reveal the underlying neurophysiology of unconscious processes, dreaming, and memory. Biological and genetic studies have added to and corrected our notions of nature/nurture and the etiology of diseases such as schizophrenia, bipolar disorder, and major depression.

At the same time these advances have created unintended consequences in the quality and effectiveness of treatment. Psychodynamic psychotherapy is often caught between the biological/medicational approaches to treatment on the one hand and the "brief, treat the symptoms" surface approaches on the other. We have watched this development unfold and fear that it will continue unabated. Damage being done to patients is difficult to measure, but highly probable. These circumstances have challenged us to outline the core characteristics of the therapist who becomes an effective listener to the melodies of the mind.

Psychotherapy works best when the therapist has experiential intelligence, that is, when he is temperamentally suited for the work, well trained, and possessed of a personality that is adaptable enough to work with most patients. These conditions are not necessarily obvious to the patient or to the therapist. Listening effectively and affectively to the melody of the mind is a goal we can only strive to approximate. How would we describe the person of the psychodynamic psychotherapist? We consider that when psychotherapy works, the therapist would generally fit the following profile.

We are thinking of a psychotherapist who has a philosophical and inquiring outlook that is emotionally and intellectually stimulated and challenged by the chance to address the complexity and variability of another human being. It is difficult for us to imagine anyone interested in practicing as a clinician, failing to be captivated by the challenge to comprehend and to grapple with the fantastic demons and the confusing and repetitive themes that invade mental life creating ominous and foreboding melodies.

Such a psychotherapist would be temperamentally suited to engage other human beings on psychological terms in a two-person therapy process and respond to the emotional distress of patients as signaled by anger, anxiety, guilt, and depression. These are some of the intolerable emotions from which patients want to be freed. Effective clinicians are not confused or discombobulated by a patient's intense emotionality or by a patient's confusion or passivity. *Emotionally, a therapist needs to be an Olympic-class athlete.*

Therapists must look for recurring themes, they must be willing to be surprised and know what to do with that surprise technically, and they must listen for the disguised variations of the same theme. Empathy for the patient is not manifested by being warm, or loving, or personal. The patient experiences the therapist as empathic when the therapist listens and observes carefully and steadily while trying to understand and to help the patient integrate the raw material of each session. Empathy for the patient means being understood in depth, not in everyway, but about the conflicts and defenses that brought the patient to therapy in the first place.

This therapist would also have a strong, academic background in a wide range of conceptual and theoretical psychiatric material. Talent, intuition, and a good temperament are the necessary but not sufficient requirements for a competent listener. One must also have useful concepts available to help make sense of the patient's conflicts. Consider the old adage, "there is nothing as practical as a good theory." Basic psychiatric knowledge, favorable personality factors, clinical experience, and an empirical approach to treatment are the four essentials for a good psychodynamic therapist.

Such a therapist would have several years of supervised clinical experience in diagnostic evaluation of the many psychiatric disorders, especially including inpatient experience. Supervised inpatient experience is essential to insure complete exposure to the full range of psychological disturbances. Clinicians who lack this inpatient diagnostic training are vulnerable to mistaking the different forms of psychological problems, underestimating or overestimating psychopathology, and inappropriately applying treatment. Inpatient experience enables clinical confidence to be applied appropriately. It also helps to diminish clinical anxiety that comes with never having seen or worked with severe psychiatric patients and their often-frightening melodies of mind.

The competent psychodynamic psychotherapist would have obtained extensive, in-depth supervision in the technique aspects of practicing psychotherapy, that is, listening, observing, clarifying, questioning, and responding in ways that are informed by an empirically established conceptual framework. Relying on intuition and flying by the seat of one's pants without empirical support is a prescription for psychotherapy that doesn't work. Winston Churchill remarked that "imagination without deep and full knowledge is a snare."[1] As Erik Erikson summarized so well, "I have nothing to offer except a way of looking at things." We think he meant to create a different and better melody.[2] This requires a sophistication in clinical theory and in technique; neither of which come without dedication and discipline. *Experiential intelligence evolves from these processes.*

Therapists need to have their own in-depth individual psychotherapy as part of their training. This avoids the pitfalls of confusing patient issues with their own. Knowing oneself is a basic prerequisite for a therapist because one's own unresolved conflicts can act as blinders and interfere with the effective use of clinical experience as well as the ability to listen. We shall elaborate these criteria for the competent psychodynamic psychotherapist in subsequent chapters.

Notes

1. Winston Churchill, *The Grand Alliance, Volume III* (Mariner Books, 1986), 516.
2. Erik Erikson, *Childhood and Society* (New York: Norton, 1963), 359.

4

When the Therapist Isn't Good Enough

Psychodynamic psychotherapy is a hard-to-learn discipline.

EXAMPLES OF PSYCHOTHERAPISTS WHO DO NOT LISTEN to the melody of the mind are everywhere. We have seen repeatedly individuals in emotional pain and misery who gain little or nothing from psychotherapy, marriages that have failed and shouldn't have, and marriages that remained intact and shouldn't have. We have seen people who have been on psychotropic medication for years and shouldn't have been as well as patients who have never been placed on psychotropic medication and should have been. The warning discordant melodies of the suicidal mind are missed. Adolescents and adults with significant histories of disturbed behavior are seen by therapists who did not recognize the dangers for the patient and for society—consider the depressed adolescents dismissed as just having a "bad attitude" and the many people who kill themselves or others even though they were on a regimen of psychotropic medication (but not properly followed or diagnosed).

There are many kinds of psychotherapists. In many states, anyone can claim to be a therapist even if he/she has no training and lacks certain necessary dimensions of personality. No licensing or certification is required to call oneself a psychotherapist. The training programs for psychiatrists, psychologists, and clinical social workers vary widely in depth and scope. Many of these programs only skim the conceptual surface when preparing their students to cope with the complexities of the human mind. Few schools urge that the students complete their own personal, individual psychotherapy as was the case several decades ago. The amount of reading and study required and the years of supervised clinical work and training have been drastically shortened, if required at all. Short and sweet psychotherapy may be cheaper, but it misses the melody of the mind, doesn't last long, and the patients are the losers.

Psychotherapists choose to work in this field for a wide variety of personal reasons. Some of those reasons are okay and some are not. There are, for example, therapists who are fascinated by the intricacies of the human mind or who feel great compassion for the human condition of an individual. They enjoy the intellectual challenge of sifting through the psychological forces and inner demons, and listening for the disharmonious melodies that underlie a person's mental state and behavior.

A 1960s film starring Sidney Poitier and Bobby Darin called *Pressure Point* shows a prison therapist played by Sidney Poitier attempting to help Bobby Darin, a convict with a violent history, cope with terrible nightmares. The therapist explores the roots of these nightmares, maintains an even, neutral attitude, and avoids letting the overt racism, hostility, and condemnation of the patient interfere with the work. The therapist is black and the convict is an American Nazi who hates non-Aryans. Despite Darin's hateful character, the therapist stays tuned to the underlying pressures that foster the nightmares. The therapist is able to set aside his own repugnance at Darin's hate and racism and uses his knowledge and training to listen to the ominous melody blaring out during each session and works to excise the demons that haunt this patient.[1]

Contrast Poitier's good-enough psychotherapist with those who take narcissistic satisfaction from feeling superior to the patient and who use the hour to extract admiration from the patient. A therapist might feel powerful because of the self-perceived advantage he has over the patient's vulnerabilities. A therapist might want affection and love from the patient. A therapist might preach to the patient or might set up contracts the patient can't keep. The motivation of the therapist is obviously an important factor in a two-person relationship therapy.

For many therapists, tolerating and exploring certain patient affects (emotions) such as shame, anger, eroticism, and guilt present a problem. Whatever the reason for a therapist having difficulty with these affects, a not good-enough psychotherapy is the result. On the one hand, as we reviewed earlier, comfort and safety are a basic requirement a therapist must provide in order for a good psychotherapy process to take place. This means that the patient must feel free to explore with the therapist anything that comes to mind without the risk of being judged or threatened.

On the other hand, if the therapist, by whatever means—verbal or nonverbal—causes the patient to feel that the therapist would be uncomfortable or critical, then the necessary and crucial safety of the psychotherapeutic process is compromised. Safety partly depends on the therapist trying to make it easy for the patient to trust.

Another patient affect that poses a challenge for the therapist is the wariness or suspicion a patient expresses by saying "Why should I pay you? The advice you gave me is just like my friends. I want some practical advice that works." If the therapist's response is inappropriate, the patient's suspicion is transformed into distrust.

In many cases the treatment is simply off-track or misguided. Therapists who lack good evaluative skills, an adequate conceptual framework, and sufficient supervised experience are unlikely to be good at listening to the melody of the mind and can leave patients in a state of despair. When the patient cannot trust the therapist, there may be more than one way of assessing the mistrust. Sometimes the patient is smart, and the therapist should not be trusted. Sometimes the delivery of the therapy process is untrustworthy. A lack of confidence and privacy will cause mistrust.

Too often in recent decades, we find that many of our patients have been to several therapists over several years and have come away with experiences that exacerbated their condition or at a minimum were unhelpful. The patients had found the courage to seek therapy with the attendant high hopes of relief from their misery. Once seriously disappointed by what they encounter, they may turn to self-help books, alternative and ineffective therapies, and other equally unhelpful activities. Their misery continues and may worsen. Relationships may remain impaired, work activity may be compromised, and the notion of relief through therapeutic effort may be discarded. Patients may be so disappointed from the first try at a therapeutic experience that should the patient decide to try therapy again, the next therapist must first undo the damage done by the first therapist!

Significant *learning disabilities* present in some adults and children are rarely ever identified by the average therapist today. Such patients were often labeled "lazy," "unmotivated," "manipulative," or "procrastinators" by teachers and family and grew up thinking of themselves in these terms. The therapist's failure to diagnose various learning deficits makes it difficult to help patients work through their largely negative self-images and low self-esteem.

One clinical example is the case of an owner of a very successful construction company who worked out many of his internal conflicts in individual psychotherapy that lasted several years. At one point midway through the process, the therapist realized that the patient's academic history of great difficulty in high school may have been the result of an undetected learning disability. At age forty-eight, the businessman was formally evaluated to determine whether or not there was some kind of language processing deficit. When the tests were concluded, the educational and learning evaluation made it clear that he did in fact have a language processing problem and indicated that the patient was well above average in intelligence.

In the session after the report from the education evaluator, the patient presented quite differently. He walked in with a broad smile, rare for him. His normally hunched shoulders were straight up, and he did not wait as was his usual pattern, for the therapist to say something. Instead, he commented, "that Dr. so and so, you know the one that you sent me to for the education evaluation, said that I had well above average intelligence based on the testing. I never would have believed it. I never did believe it. I can't tell you how much better I feel just knowing that." All his life he thought he was not very smart, and his self-esteem had always been poor in spite of his obvious accomplishments in conducting a complicated business establishment and making a great deal of money.

Some patients are suffering from serious psychiatric conditions that are not recognized by therapists who lack psychiatric inpatient experience. Mood disorders and latent psychotic disorders, especially in adolescents, are often misperceived as part of the patient's core personality instead of a psychiatric condition. The melody full of confusion and anguish is not heard. The treatment is ineffective or worse because a serious mental disturbance is undetected, the therapy misapplied, and the need for psychotropic medications is not recognized. Underscoring this point is the fact, for example, that depressive disorders are notoriously under-diagnosed across the country. Therapists and school systems share the blame for missing the signs and symptoms of this most common and treatable psychiatric condition.

As with learning disabilities, the manifest symptoms of most depressive disorders in adolescents (slipping academic work, irritability, detachment, boredom, and so on) are most likely to be perceived by professionals who should know better as "bad attitude." There are always underlying reasons for the symptomatic behaviors. Labels such as "lazy," "procrastinating," and "manipulating" are not causes, but symptoms! Similarly, substance abuse, addictions, anorexia, bulimia, phobias, panic attacks, social ineptitude, and a host of other conditions are symptoms not causes. Of course, issues of character pathology may make diagnosis difficult. Sometimes, only a lengthy course of treatment will help to identify and to work with character pathology that may contribute to these symptoms. But our ideal therapist will have the fortitude and perseverance to stay the course.

Note

1. 1962 Movie, *Pressure Point* (MGM).

5
Authenticity

> The psychodynamic psychotherapist cares about the patient, but not too much.

THE CORNERSTONE OF GOOD PSYCHOTHERAPY IS AUTHENTICITY. The interior of a person has a particular and specific feel to it. Humans seem to have some vague sense of the interior of another person—a kind of rudimentary psychological attunement perhaps of evolutionary significance. Listening to the melody of the mind requires that the therapist be able to resonate with this interior and recognize an individual's feeling state as coming from within the person, not as a reaction to outside events. If the patient's behavior is seen as a reaction to the environment, the tendency will be to concentrate on the environment rather than on the feeling state of the patient as in "yes, your anxiety has been a reaction to your work situation, but you have been an anxious man all your life, correct?"

Organizing and clarifying comments from the experientially intelligent therapist usually tend to enlist the patient's observing mental functions, at least initially. But if patient and therapist continue to concentrate on the environment, the patient never glimpses his interior state and neither does the therapist.

It's quite easy to become close to an individual that a therapist sees in the office on a regular basis. The social situation becomes comfortable and nonthreatening. Each person likes the other person and believes because the exterior functions of office, time, and money are in their proper places, that psychotherapy is occurring. These exterior functions are necessary but not sufficient for psychotherapy. These exterior functions provide a necessary scaffolding for authentic psychological growth and development to take place. If a feeling of authenticity is lacking in the patient-therapist pair, good psychotherapy does not develop.

A sense of trust in the therapist is a prerequisite for authenticity to be part of psychotherapy. When a senior colleague is asked to consult on a case that seems to be stagnating, very often the patient will say, "I just can't tell my therapist everything. I would be too scared"—or more benignly, "I don't think that (painful) issue is very important," or "it's too private." One winces when one hears "my therapist is like a family member." That statement reveals that the relationship with the therapist is most likely non-therapeutic, because we usually don't tell our family members all of our interior thoughts and feelings. We usually tell family members enough about what we think to keep the family on an even keel. As a matter of fact, when a family member talks too much about his/her feelings about another family member, those words may be turned to a hurtful and destructive use particularly if the words are attached to powerful emotions.

Many therapists believe that an overly personal involvement with a patient builds trust and an authentic relationship. We are not sure that it does. The patient wants to feel that the therapist is objective and has a balanced perspective on what he is telling her. If the patient feels the therapist is too close, then he believes that the therapist cannot be objective and therefore cannot be trusted. Under these circumstances the patient will not be able to develop an authentic sense of himself in the therapist's office. Authenticity is an intangible but critical requirement for the intuitively astute, psychodynamic psychotherapist.

The psychotherapist must maintain an interest in the patient without too much closeness, and that is much harder to do than it is to write about. An authentic psychotherapist will care about the patient but not care too much. He/she will be an interested observer and commentator but not an intrusive judge with authoritative directions.

The psychodynamic psychotherapist tries to see the person in the disguise of patient and to separate the person out of the morass of the symptom complex and the cacophony of the discordant melodies. The therapist recognizes the person's potential as hidden by the disguise of the irrational, uncomfortable behavior of his overt presentation. A good psychotherapist keeps the categories and complaints alongside the person who has them and recognizes that these categories and complaints are not intrinsic to the authentic person within, sitting in the room, yet is nowhere to be found. Therapists must allow patients to find themselves and find their own synchronous melodies of mind.

II

THE NECESSARY CLINICAL KNOWLEDGE

6

Adequate Theoretical/ Conceptual Frameworks

The psychodynamic psychotherapist listens for the melody of the unconscious.

ONE OF THE MOST COMMON REASONS FOR THE THERAPIST FAILING to listen effectively to the melody of the mind has much to do with poor diagnostic/evaluative skills—the consequence of inadequate training. A therapist relying on intuitive skills alone tends to force an emotional discharge of his own unconscious conflicts into the patient's psychological space. So the patient is used for the defensive purpose of gratifying the therapist. The therapist's training has not provided enough comprehensive, empirically based concepts to help in developing the experiential intelligence one must acquire in order to understand and work with the patient's melody. Of course the therapist's own inner conflicts should be resolved by personal intensive psychodynamic psychotherapy as well. We will discuss this point more fully later.

In addition to a therapist's weak theoretical frameworks, his training deficiencies also prevent good-enough psychotherapy. We are concerned about how a clinician can be effective in separating severe psychopathology from garden-variety neurotic conflict or from reactions to childhood trauma without an extended period of inpatient psychiatric experience or other equivalent, supervised experience—perhaps three to five years. After all, most people who are experiencing the onset of a disorder in the mood disorder spectrum, disorders in the schizophrenic spectrum, or other serious, potentially psychotic disorders do not always present as having a severe disturbance. Nor are patients with serious personality disturbances readily recognized without extensive training. One must be exposed to and supervised in treating these conditions in order to recognize the underlying psychopathology and not confuse them with something else.

Descriptive Psychiatry

There are two major systems one can use to evaluate the patient, and they are not mutually exclusive. Psychodynamic therapists must be familiar with the strength and weaknesses of both. One system is known as descriptive psychiatry. In this system attention is paid to a wide variety of signs, symptoms, and behaviors of the patient. The signs, symptoms, and behaviors are then collected into meaningful clusters—diagnoses attuned to the narrowed down categories of the Diagnostic and Statistical Manual of the American Psychiatric Association [DSM-IV-TR]. The DSM-IV-TR is quite helpful for many disorders, especially those having a biological substrate such as schizophrenia, bipolar disorder, major depression, and organic disorders. The system is also helpful for recognizing and organizing symptom patterns such as in anxiety states, paranoid states, phobias, and perversions.

Unfortunately, the manual does not provide a way of understanding the etiology of disease nor the treatment of specific diseases. Nor does it allow for a continuum of disorder, tending to sacrifice a wide dimensionality for the simplicity of narrow categorical diagnoses. The insurance industry has relied on the DSM coding report of the treating mental health professional to establish a basis for payment of services.

It is relatively easy to assess the cluster of symptoms and behaviors with which a patient presents. Anyone with good observational skills and good reference skills can develop the ability to prepare a numeric diagnostic code. But the conceptual framework is limited to diagnosis as developed statistically—that's why it's called the diagnostic and *statistical* manual. Statistical diagnosis does not necessarily provide a clinical path to treat an individual.

Because the DSM-IV-TR is based on observable activity, and is not an explanatory guide to symptoms, the causality and the spectral nature of most disorders are not taken into account. Yet clinical judgment often depends on understanding causality and variation. Whether or not to hospitalize a suicidal patient may depend, for example, on why the patient is presently suicidal. In the rating instruments widely used, such as the Hamilton rating scale or the many other depression and anxiety rating scales, a person checking the various points is the patient. Thus, the data are not objective but subjective. A person's affect strongly influences his/her cognition and vice versa. We are not surprised therefore that the accuracy from subjective ratings is limited.

Psychodynamic Psychiatry

Psychodynamic psychotherapy, on the other hand, seeks to use a complex clinical framework to help *explain* the causes of the patient's signs, symptoms, and behaviors. This is done by applying the rich psychodynamic concepts of mental functioning to reveal the substrate of most human psychopathology—what are the patient's underlying conflicts, defensive postures, and armoring; how are affects and impulses regulated; what are the core elements of the patient's identity; what is the quality of the patient's object relations; how well are these aspects of mental functioning integrated. In essence, this system tries to understand what makes the patient "tick."

The Psychodynamic Diagnostic Manual (PDM) published by the Alliance of Psychoanalytic Organizations is "based on neuroscience, treatment outcome research, and other empirical investigations"[1] and embedded in a rich, psychodynamic scaffolding. It is a diagnostic framework that attempts to characterize an individual's full range of functioning—the depth as well as the surface of emotional, cognitive, and social patterns. As we suggested in an earlier section, unconscious motives are the source of much human behavior and internal conflict. A developmental history is clinically necessary for a fuller grasp of these motives and conflicts. The psychodynamic psychotherapist holds that "the child is father of the man"—William Wadsworth said it plainly.

A clinical conceptual framework in psychodynamic psychotherapy is much harder to develop and even harder to understand. (The PDM is an outline of such a framework.) The same set of symptoms in two different patients with the same diagnosis may result in two different therapeutic interventions with two different sets of results. To make the situation even more problematic, we may not be able to predict from the first diagnostic interview what patient will fall into which therapeutic category.

Any clinician who has spent any time working in a hospital knows that different patients with the same illness heal differently and may have different outcomes. But many psychotherapists today haven't had inpatient experience and need to develop their clinical framework through their clinical experience outside the hospital. This is a daunting task because as we noted earlier, the inexperienced psychotherapist has not been exposed to the spectrum of symptom clusters or the range of therapeutic responses for a variety of interventions.

The psychotherapist must be capable of fully evaluating the extent and nature of a patient's condition, appreciate the patient's individual psychology, and actively seek an explanation for the patient's symptoms and behaviors.

We cannot emphasize enough how important it is for the therapist to make careful distinctions so that diagnostic efforts are a help and not a hindrance to effective treatment. Anxiety for example, can be seen as a disorder in some cases. But anxiety is a symptom in most cases. Not looking for the unconscious pressures that induce the anxiety increases the chances that the psychotherapy will not work. Anxiety is a symptom just as a fever is a symptom. We do not talk of "fever disorders." We should only be talking of anxiety disorders in a very limited number of cases. Some people tend to inherit a tendency to be anxious but in most of us it is created, either by a current real-life situation, by early developmental experiences still affecting us unconsciously, or by certain severe psychiatric disorders. In a few cases there may be a genetic vulnerability. The same point can be made about a number of so-called disorders such as eating disorders, a large percentage of addictive disorders, oppositional disorders, impulse disorders, and adjustment disorders.

Cassie is an example of inadequate treatment intervention and the need for breadth and depth in clinical concepts and training in order to do psychodynamic psychotherapy.

Between the ages of sixteen and thirty-four Cassie was seen by at least a half-dozen therapists and had been hospitalized twice because of strong suicidal feelings. There was a long history of acting out behavior, promiscuity, impulse buying, overeating, and obesity. Her background included significant family conflict and childhood despair. She had evolved a passive-dependent pattern of behavior in her relationships as an early reaction to a controlling, rejecting, narcissistic mother. She was overweight and had some medical problems. Cassie was very smart and had wanted to attend medical school. She couldn't quite pull it off. She did, however, manage to win a graduate degree in social work and over the years, despite her struggles, became a highly regarded professional.

Cassie was psychologically minded and knew she needed help to control her episodes of despair and chronic impulsive episodes. So she sought help, and over the years she had seen therapists who attempted to be supportive, gave her advice, and listened sympathetically. She was an excellent reporter of her symptoms and behavior. But none of the clinicians seemed to have listened to her discordant but functional harmonies and surmised the nature of her complex condition.

Cassie saw two therapists who worked together. One was a "massage therapist," and the other conducted "rebirthing therapy" and "energy field therapy." These therapists determined that Cassie must have been sexually abused because of her response to the massage therapy. So they referred her to a therapist who worked with her in a group setting. He determined that the best way to help her with the supposedly repressed sexual history of abuse that never happened was to lay on top of her in the group and tell her to "push me away." Apparently he had some notion of how to help a victim with this technique.

In terms of conceptual knowledge, one is reminded of the old saw "if all you have is a hammer, everybody looks like a nail."

Cassie's first hospitalization, unfortunately, did not result in a careful assessment and identification of the problem. After discharge she was given the diagnosis of borderline personality disorder. It is dismaying to realize that none of these half-dozen therapists and two hospitalizations resulted in an adequate evaluation of her condition and appropriate treatment rendered. These clinicians seemed to have missed the boat. It is hard to escape the conclusion that they were ill equipped because they lacked the knowledge conceptually to understand what they were seeing in Cassie, to be attuned to her repetitive melody of inner chaos. These were not good therapeutic interventions.

Certainly the therapist who treated Cassie by having her play at pushing him away was employing his own fantasy strategies for treatment. He seems to have been unacquainted with common clinical concepts regarding trauma, with clinical concepts of intrapsychic conflict, and with concepts derived from developmental psychology. It may feel good to say "push me away." There is a momentary sense of empowerment for the patient and the therapist. But this is not good psychotherapy.

For example, Cassie had significant interpersonal relations issues surrounding her developing years and relations with her parents. She employed passive-dependent attitudes to modulate her anxiety stemming from those years and used certain foods to manage the feelings of loneliness and longings. Knowledgeable therapists with an adequate conceptual framework in child development should have recognized the conflicts created by her childhood experiences and explored these issues with her.

We also find it hard to explain how the hospital therapists could have discharged her with a borderline diagnosis. Cassie was clearly suffering with a bipolar disorder. All the signs and symptoms had been present since the age of sixteen.

Cassie was an articulate narrator of her condition. She once arrived at her psychotherapy session and announced, "I think my meds [for mania] need adjusting." Asked why, she replied that she had just spent a thousand dollars on a vacuum cleaner. When the therapist replied that it did not seem an unreasonable amount for a quality vacuum, she replied, "Yes, but I have a central vacuuming system in my condo." If a bipolar disorder as clear as Cassie's isn't recognized in a psychiatric facility, we fear the deterioration in the learning and application of the necessary conceptual frameworks. When the therapist is listening to the melody emanating from the patient's pain, the patient can then learn to use psychologic concepts to understand and modulate her own behavior.

To put it succinctly, too many therapists who should have clinical knowledge derived from a thorough grounding in psychological, social, biological, and philosophical frames of reference, apparently do not.

Another danger from inadequate conceptual knowledge is seen when a therapist attributes one patient's issues to one set of causes when another set is just as probable and remains unexplored. For example, it is all too common for therapists to accept, uncritically, a patient's complaints about a spouse, parent, or child without fully vetting the patient's own contribution. Many a patient has presented in the therapist's office saying my spouse, or parent, or child is an awful, mean, sick person, and tells stories to illustrate. Sometimes it is the case, but sometimes it is not. Borderline and narcissistically disordered patients often are disruptive and difficult to live with. The other family members if interviewed might say, "I feel like I'm going crazy." The therapist can't really help if accurate distinctions are not made.

Sometimes what looks like an insecure attachment may instead really reflect a defensive reaction, that is, a separation problem that the person has attempted to solve by reaction to the primary attachment figure. John was a man who was successful in business, had many friends, and several close ones that he had had for most of his life. His wife complained that he was avoiding her and disinterested in the family. The marriage counselor had suggested his fear of intimacy stemmed from an insecure primary attachment. This is a bold statement based on the wife's complaints and a "logical" cause and effect way of thinking. A good psychodynamic psychotherapist is aware that in science, causality and correlation are two different things but they can be conflated.

Since John had a rather ordinary early childhood with an intact family and an unremarkable relationship with parents and siblings, we would be hard-pressed to agree with such a bold statement about him. We might also add that the counselor had been tactless, siding with the wife and pathologizing the husband, creating an atmosphere of blame in the couple.

By the time John was seen by a therapist, the marriage was ended thanks to a sophisticated legal adversarial situation. The work was relatively easy from this point. John needed to recognize that in his early childhood relationships, he was the eldest child and wanted to please his mother who was a little too controlling for a little boy who wanted only to ride his bicycle and play with his friends. Conflicts with his mother resulted in John burying himself in computer games.

When he got on the bus heading for college, he vowed he would never go back home for an extended period. John had to work too hard psychologically in order to feel independent. By the time he fell in love with his wife, he was very cautious about women being "too possessive." He tried very hard to keep his distance from his wife because she could be "so controlling." "When I was six years old I thought my mother and father belonged to me just the way my dog did. I could sometimes control my dog but I couldn't control my wife." So what was creative rebellion on the part of a six-year-old turned out to be cruel dismissal on the part of a thirty-six-year-old.

John first came to the therapist's office believing that he was the product of poor parenting and had therefore developed an insecure attachment which in turn caused him to be fearful of intimacy. He was motivated and psychologically minded so that after about a year of once-weekly treatment he developed a more relaxed notion of himself that encompassed understanding his need to fight against women who were "too controlling." He understood that his psychological defenses were useful to help him protect himself. He could be more self-reflective and more willing to view women in more varied ways. The therapist, because of her training, used the sign of the increased self-reflection as a diagnostic indicator of defensive attachment as distinguished from insecure attachment.

Oftentimes, our patients come from backgrounds where the parent–child relationship may have been problematic. Herb was a man who had been brought up in a very suspicious environment. When he went to public school and learned about the realities of magical thinking and went home to confront his parents, he was taunted with "oh you're not so smart, after all you haven't seen the things we have." As he grew up, he learned not to believe anything his parents told him. But he relied so much on himself that he turned around and believed everyone else in the world was stupid. It would be hard not to conclude that this was an overreaction to his parents telling him he wasn't so smart. His parents taunting and denigrating verbal behavior metamorphosed into an independent but arrogant and narcissistic personality style.

Herb was a man who became abrasive, arrogant, and aggressive. He also became very, very rich. In his business dealings he was known to be ruthless. In his family he was despotic. His children hated him. His wife finally left him. Herb died an embittered man never understanding how his isolating and narcissistically based defenses deprived him of intimate relationships. The therapist did not consider that Herb had an attachment disorder but rather that he had narcissistic problems set in motion by his intense need to be independent in his awareness of himself and others at a premature age. Without understanding the causes of Herb's attitudes and behavior it would be easy to confound him with someone with an insecure attachment problem instead of a character issue with narcissistic defenses. A psychotherapist, listening carefully, would have felt an emotional resonance with the melody of this patient's narcissism and would have detected the rhapsody of self-centeredness in the patient.

When considering a patient for a diagnosis of personality disorder, we are on a very slippery slope. Many borderline and narcissistic patients for example, have had at least one very narcissistic parent. There was no gleam in the parent's eye for the child. The child had no way in seeing herself reflected in the parent's facial expressions. Ironically we might be able to say that this kind of patient has an insecure primary attachment. Of course we know that borderline patients may have primary attachment problems. So we might say that a patient with a borderline personality might have had a narcissistic parent and developed, among other things, insecure attachment disorder. But all patients who have these attachment problems are not borderline personalities. Therapists must remember that correlation is not causality.

Borderline patients vary in the severity of their disorder, but most have complicated issues that can sometimes be confused with other disorders such as impulsivity, dreadful emptiness, and identity diffusion. They are often misdiagnosed as depressed patients, bipolar patients, and childhood trauma patients. Of course any patient may fit two or more clinical entities. A psychodynamic psychotherapist has to be educated and ready to make these diagnostic discriminations.

Note

1. Alliance of Psychoanalytic Organizations, *Psychodynamic Diagnostic Manual* (PDM) (2006).

7

Multiple Points of View

Romance, Comedy, Irony, Tragedy

THERE IS AN OLD SAYING, "TOO SOON WE GET OLD AND TOO LATE SMART." The saying has a cousin called, "I attended the school of hard knocks." The point, we think, is that wisdom comes with age and not fast enough to avoid many mistakes. But mistakes are an inevitable part of tempering a therapist and imparting a fuller and richer appreciation for the lives of others that informs the therapist's observations and responses to the patient.

Schafer (1976) proposed that there are four larger perspectives or points of view about reality found in human experience—romance, comedy, tragedy, and irony.[1] Psychotherapy at the core is a special form of knowing about human existence and has its roots in the humanities as well as science.

There are also many psychologic points of view—developmental and relational, neuroscientific and genetic, psychodynamic and psychosocial. Psychotherapy might also be likened to a microscope with many different lenses for peering more deeply into the human mind.

A competent psychotherapist applies his experiential intelligence in part based on these or similar, internalized points of view. Such a therapist has an expansive, studied, psychological armamentarium. He works with Schafer's four humanistic visions of reality, at least intuitively if not theoretically. These psychologic points of view and visions of reality are essential for a therapist to sort out the unconscious feelings and thoughts that underlie the internal conflicts making the patient miserable.

A good therapist need not have experienced everything their patients have experienced. An oncologist doesn't need to have had cancer to treat it. However, it is essential that they recognize such experiences as part of life and have a real "open-mindedness" (Lear, 1998)[2] about them.

Familiarity with art, literature, history, and science is essential. Without a base of knowledge of literature, history, myths, and social/cultural themes, the therapist might not appreciate much of the material presented by the patient. It is not too much to expect that a therapist who wishes to listen to the melodies of mind and work with the psychological aspects of another human being be familiar with the great poets and writers whose sharp intuitions have been observing fellow humans for centuries. Their work is so critical in shaping our sense of reality and our understanding of the patient's life narrative that we cannot do without their perspectives of romance, comedy, tragedy, and irony in everyday life. There is little room in the practice of psychotherapy for rigid, narrow-minded psychotherapists, or superficial psychotherapists, or arrogant narcissistic therapists. It would be difficult for such therapists to have the variety of viewpoints needed to help a patient because the melodies of mind are many and complex.

How do these "points of view" affect the practice of psychotherapy? A good psychotherapist must be able to empathize authentically with a patient who may be enduring emotional pain. An appreciation of life's tragic, ironic, and comedic elements are fundamental to this process.

The case of Alexandra, a thirty-seven-year-old divorced mother of two, is illustrative. Alexandra was a tall and attractive, yet thin and gaunt-looking hospice nurse. Her complaints were of being overwhelmed. Specifically, she found herself unable to cope with her feelings of frustration about her difficulties with her children as they reached puberty. The therapist decided that Alexandra was depressed and sent her to a pharmacologist who prescribed antidepressants. After four years of supportive psychotherapy and a number of antidepressant medications, she felt only marginally better. Alexandra finally sought a second opinion.

The second therapist took a lengthy history. Alexandra was the youngest of three girls—eight years younger than one sister and eleven years younger than another, the eldest. The family was described as rather taciturn and not given too much in the way of emotional expression. Her father set the emotional and organizational rhythm of the family. She was the baby and very close to mom. Apparently mom found great satisfaction in doting on Alexandra.

When Alexandra was almost fourteen, mom had arranged for her to go to a summer camp for three weeks, and Alexandra was very excited. Mom had been ill and was scheduled for an operation just before Alexandra left. Since the surgery was considered routine, Alexandra went to camp. As luck would have it, mom died from a staph infection following the operation a week after Alexandra left. The family (her father, two sisters, and a brother-in-law) organized the funeral and burial, and decided to let Alexandra stay at camp for the remaining two-and-one-half weeks. She was informed of her mother's death and burial on the two-and-one-half-hour ride home from the summer camp two weeks later. It was presented to her calmly and unemotionally. At home life resumed with little discussion. There was no acknowledgment of such a great loss. (See Madelon Sprengnether's personal story in this regard, *Crying at the Movies*, 2001).[3]

Alexandra graduated high school and then married. In the next eight years she worked and raised her family. She divorced her husband after eight years mainly because of his "unavailability." He had little to do with his children after the divorce. As the children reached puberty, life at home became more turbulent. Alexandra found herself unable to set limits, to persuade the children to behave, or to engage them in an effective and constructive manner. The youngsters argued, complained about everything, and were generally sullen and easily irritated.

A further evaluation of Alexandra's situation was made on the basis of a combination of assessment of empirical data and a sense of Alexandra's life as built on the experience of a tragedy. On the one hand there was the empirical data—information on the family history, the ages of the children and the divorce, the observable nonverbal elements of Alexandra's presentation, the reactions of the children in sessions with the mother. On the other hand there was the sense of the tragedy and irony in the mother's life—the incredible behavior of Alexandra's family of origin around her mother's death and now Alexandra's apparent flat emotional presentation of the story. Yet her current work as a hospice nurse caring for dying people seemed a twist of fate. The emergence of problems with her children as they approached the age of her own adolescent experience of her mother's death underscored the unresolved tragedy in Alexandra's life. The death of a parent may be a developmental shock that prevents an adult from bringing important "executive functions" to parenting skills. Alexandra didn't have her own mother in her psychologic makeup when her children reached the age of fourteen. It's not clear whether or not Alexandra was repeating in some way her adolescent experience with her father when she chose an unavailable man or was re-creating, in her marriage, her early experience of losing her mother, as an attempt to finally master her emotional grief. Perhaps it was both.

A good psychodynamic therapist knows that from a developmental point of view, Alexandra's sense of reality, that is, feeling oneself to be solid, real, and self-connected was affected by the family's handling of her mother's death. Alexandra's melody was reflected in her somber, flattened emotional presentation. Her narrative style was vague, and her visual presentation seemed will-o'-the-wisp. The therapist could almost hear the music of mourning, the faint notes of a dirge in Alexandra's voice, perhaps an unconscious reaction to having been denied even attendance at her mother's funeral.

From an object relations point of view, Alexandra's ability to relate to others in intimate fashion had been damaged. The therapist would know from the point of view of conflict–defense concepts that Alexandra would have trouble as her children reached her historic age at the time of her mother's death. She would then be able to help her comprehend the emotionally enormous consequences of her family of origin's decision not to bring her home from camp and their general intolerance of emotional distress.

Sensitivity to the irony and tragedy of Alexandra's experiences were critical ingredients in her treatment. Listening to her melody of frozen grief and despair, it should have been easy to see how diminished her life had become. It would require not only her awareness of the impact of the tragic childhood circumstances, but a calm, empathic, attentive, and mostly silent therapist while she absorbed and integrated the emotional material involved. The therapist's sense of the tragic needed to be transmitted into affect that the patient could feel.

Working at a hospice giving dying patients care and nurturance reflected the missed opportunity to be with her own mother at death. Hospice work draws deeply on the psychologic resources of the caregiver. What was left for Alexandra's own children? Surely Alexandra had identified with her own father and chose a profession where she could rationally emulate his emotionless relationship with children. Thoughtful, understanding interventions might help temper the intense anguish of her finally accepting the tragic component of her life. Alexandra needed to expand her perspective on her experience. She needed to feel grief, resignation, and sadness about the tragedy rather than a freeze on the feelings that denial brings. Sometimes a freeze on feelings stops everything—no grasp of parenting, no sense of well-being, and no sense of intimate relationships.

After the material has been explored, the therapist must sit with her in silence and in empathy and, in accord with Winnicott's point of view, the notion of two people "*being alone together*."[4] But the therapist listened in the silence to the slow, sometimes tortured melody of frozen feelings thawing. The therapist's appreciation of tragedy and irony were needed for a good therapeutic outcome.

Notes

1. Roy Schafer, "The Psychoanalytic Vision of Reality," in *A New Language for Psychoanalysis* (New Haven, Conn.: Yale University Press, 1976), chap. 3.

2. Lear, *Open Minded*, 84.
3. Madelon Sprengnether, *Crying at the Movies: A Film Memoir* (Graywolf Press, 2001).
4. D. W. Winnicott, "The Capacity to Be Alone," *International Journal of Psycho Analysis* 39 (1958): 416–20.

8

Supervised Experience in Diagnosing and Treating

The therapist may not privilege any desire over the growth and development of the patient.

A GOOD PSYCHOTHERAPY SUPERVISOR IS THE GUARDIAN of the supervisory relationship with the inexperienced but hopeful future psychodynamic psychotherapist student. There is an artisan's approach to supervision—a passing along intellectual and emotional ways of being and listening to the student of psychotherapy. Often there is a parallel process that goes on between the supervisor–student psychotherapist pair and the psychotherapist–patient pair. Identifications, imitations, and experiences are passed along without the necessary awareness or acknowledgment. The student psychotherapist unconsciously and consciously emulates the supervisor.

Like a fine film director who allows the actors to move into cognitive and emotional areas that need to be explored and nuanced, so does an able psychotherapy supervisor. Such a supervisor will listen to the supervisee with the hope of guiding him into listening to the patient in ways that privilege the patient. Too often, the supervisor is listening to himself, putting an authoritative stamp on the listening of the student so that the supervisee learns to listen to the supervisor instead of to the patient. An effective supervisor will teach the supervisee to listen to the patient by example so that the parallel process developing between the supervisor and supervisee will be brought into the treatment process between supervisee and patient.

The psychotherapy student should go through a developmental process under the direction of the supervisor. A student starts with anxiety and lack of listening and technical skills. As the student continues, implementing supervision with academic knowledge and personal psychotherapy, the student's anxiety should decrease. A decrease in anxiety will help the student to be less self-referential during supervision, for example, what does the supervisor think of me, and become skillful at listening to the melody of the patient's mind. Then the supervision will take the patient into account first and the student-therapist second. As the supervision continues, transference and countertransference issues become more central to the supervision thereby replacing the ordinary week to week narrative by the student of surface phenomena in the treatment process.

A personal experience in psychodynamic psychotherapy is a critical requirement for a future psychodynamic psychotherapist. Good supervision depends on the student having a personal therapist (not the supervisor) to explore the student's own mind and emotions. Without that personal psychotherapy experience the supervision may slip into counseling and authoritative didactics or worse yet, a quasi-treatment situation. We would rather see supervision as a didactic seminar than a treatment situation resulting from a boundary violation of supervision.

The Melody of the Unconscious

Neutrality in supervision must be in reference to the psychological conflict. It is difficult to be neutral in a relationship between two people. If there is no confidentiality the psychological conflict cannot be listened for and interpreted from a neutral position. Without neutrality, the supervisee does not learn to listen and will not therefore be able to hear the melody. It is the melody of the unconscious, listened to with care and within a clinical framework, which allows the therapist to make interpretations that will move the process of the therapy forward. A therapist may feel reassured that he is following the rules of the supervisor, and then the compliant patient may also be reassured that the rules of the therapist-student are being followed. So the autonomy of the therapist-student and of the patient are not achieved. In fact, if the patient happens to be noncompliant, the patient may get worse—a not uncommon occurrence.

There is a tendency in life to wish to remain with things that are familiar and secure whether or not those circumstances are beneficial. The patient wants to remain socially connected to the therapist. When the therapist is interested in a social connection to the patient, a true psychotherapeutic relationship cannot be created. Therapeutic skills often mitigate against the desire to connect to the patient. A psychologic dialogue and uncomfortable questions and observations preclude a comfortable social relationship. Pretence to a limited degree influences most social relationships. A therapeutic relationship strives to minimize social pretense. The patient learns to replace familiar, comfortable styles that have been unsuccessful with more adaptive styles. Therapeutic skill enhances the psychologic autonomy of the patient rather than the social comfort of the relationship.

But the regressive, comforting social pull makes a therapist feel the dependent need of the patient and the wish to overconnect may be at a cost of sensible diagnosis, treatment plan, and therapeutic intervention. The balancing of the therapeutic desire to connect with minimal ordinary social behavior defines an important aspect of the psychodynamic therapist.

The capacity to wait is an ability to withhold, not act, not engage, not connect, and not initiate or intervene. The capacity to wait must be developed in anyone wishing to engage in psychodynamically oriented psychotherapy. A beginning student emulates the supervisor by being silent. This silence is often the first step in learning to wait. The next step is to learn to listen to what is being said, as well as to what is not being said and to carefully decide whether or not to intervene at some point. Without the development of the capacity to wait, the student will never understand the art of listening. The supervisor must explicitly teach this capacity to the student. In a different setting waiting capacity may also be recognized as the absence of desire. Neither the supervisor nor the therapist-student may privilege the desire over the growth and development of the patient.

It is easy for the therapist to say with some rationale that his only desire is that the patient get better. Such altruistic desires however may interfere with the therapeutic process, so the desire must be held in mind along with the social wish to connect to the patient. Without the capacity to wait, there cannot be neutrality. The supervisor is not neutral in regard to the supervisee or the patient but must try to achieve neutrality in regard to the psychological conflict that we are privileged to witness and explore. Neutrality will help prevent enactments on the part of the supervisee and the patient. Neutrality will allow the supervisee to verbalize therapeutic interventions rather than enact personal reactions to the patient. In our view a supervisor should endorse a position of neutrality. A personal didactic treatment for the psychotherapy student is mandatory for the student to explore her own unconscious fantasies that prevent a neutral position with regard to the patient's psychological conflict.

When a position of neutrality is lost, the therapist is more likely to become involved in enactments which may or may not be therapeutic. Sometimes an enactment, if minor, gives the therapist additional information about the relationship between patient and therapist. Sometimes an enactment may be a major boundary violation and either cause harm to the patient, or disrupt the treatment process. For example, if a therapist changes the flowers on her desk to please a new patient with a particular aesthetic sensibility, we believe that the therapist needs to become self-aware of the significance of this small behavior. The behavior should be examined. The therapist might recognize a minor enactment that allowed her to explore her wish to feel that she has good taste. If she had instead asked the patient to bring new flowers since the patient didn't like hers, it would be a boundary violation, albeit an innocent enough one. Examples of boundary violations that involve expensive gifts, money arrangements, or sexual misconduct are hazardous to the treatment process.

Ethical considerations are part of understanding the capacity to wait and the exercise of neutrality. It is unethical to have sex with the patient under any and all circumstances. But it is a boundary violation that is not uncommon and usually occurs without a capacity to wait and without neutrality. Often severe boundary violations occur when the therapist is isolated. That is not to say that boundary violations do not occur under the best of circumstances. But they occur less frequently and with less catastrophe if the therapist has had adequate supervision and personal didactic psychotherapy.

9

Spectrum Disorders—Schizophrenia, Mood Disorders

"I never promised you a rose garden."

—Frieda Fromm-Reichmann

WE BELIEVE IT IMPORTANT TO DISCUSS the following spectrum disorders for a psychodynamic psychotherapist's consideration regarding the treatment of patients in the schizophrenic spectrum and the mood disorder spectrum.

Patients in the Schizophrenic Spectrum

The schizophrenic spectrum is composed of the full blown clinical disorders that include the paranoid, catatonic, disorganized, residual and undifferentiated schizophrenias as well as the subclinical (subsyndromal, subdiagnostic) syndromes that include schizotypical, schizoid, and paranoid personality disorders, and certain peculiar personality features. The latter subclinical types are much more prevalent in the general population than the schizophrenias themselves. Early recognition of risk cases and mild cases is decisive for prophylaxis. Research into the genetics of schizophrenia has been going on for over one hundred years.

There is a decades old lack of interest in the United States in psychotherapeutic endeavors with patients in the schizophrenic spectrum. Most of the psychotherapy being done with such patients is cognitive behavior therapy and is being more actively done in Europe than the United States. Prior to the employment of cognitive behavioral therapy for the treatment of schizophrenic patients, most of the therapy with these patients was carried out by psychodynamic psychotherapists.

The most famous of these was the psychoanalytic psychotherapist who was made famous by a book written by one of her ex-patients, the title of which was *I Never Promised You a Rose Garden.*[1] The therapist, of course, was Frieda Fromm-Reichmann. She worked in the mid-twentieth century at the famous Chestnut Lodge in Rockville, Maryland. In those days, it was common for very smart, dedicated psychoanalytic psychotherapists to conduct extensive and intensive psychotherapy with almost all psychiatric disorders. Today the number of such practitioners as Frieda Fromm-Reichmann is small indeed, perhaps a few hundred in the whole of the United States and the western world. The best kept secret in mental health today is about how successful these amazing practitioners are with such patients. Their numbers are shrinking each year.

There certainly are many, many clinicians who treat patients in the schizophrenic spectrum, but most of this is done with medication, group, and supportive psychotherapy, and not in-depth psychotherapy. The employment of cognitive behavioral therapy has been a more recent phenomenon perhaps for the past couple of decades. Cognitive behavior therapy attempts to integrate the concept that psychosis is derived from a series of stress-induced misinterpretations into the patient's way of thinking.

We think it is important to explore the question of whether or not a good psychodynamic psychotherapist should engage in psychotherapy with a patient in the schizophrenic spectrum. We think it is also important to discuss the cognitive behavioral approach of integrating the patient's misinterpretations in thinking but not the patient's affective confusion. These are the two issues. Should psychodynamic psychotherapists engage in the psychotherapy of schizophrenic patients and if so, can they do the work of a psychodynamic psychotherapist if they do not treat the patients' affective confusion? The work of treating the affective confusion requires that the therapist be able to work with "primary process" material. The detailed nature of engaging a patient's primary process is beyond the scope of this book. Suffice it to say that if one is uneasy around primary process levels of emotion and confusion, we do not recommend that he/she treat these patients except through a more cognitive/behavioral approach.

From a dynamic point of view, a thought disorder not only involves illogical splits from reality, but also the concomitant emotional (affective) disturbances that relate to the breaks in reality. Sometimes, someone with a thought disorder is disturbed manifestly in only certain areas of his life. With the help of the psychopharmacotherapy and psychotherapy, the patient may be able to contain the thought disorder to a more narrow field. As the patient deteriorates over time, with or without professional help the field of illness broadens considerably. The breaks with reality may then be manifested in many areas of the person's life. The wider the encompassing field of illness, the more difficult it will be to treat.

The psychotherapy depends on the therapist being able to find a comfortable point of interest that the patient and therapist can share. The therapist's affect must be genuinely engaged. Sometimes the point of interest can be music, art, books, and/or plays. One therapist remembers being engaged around apple pie with one of her schizophrenic patients. At that time, the patient could not connect to members of her family, could not adequately bathe nor manage the household. From apple pie the therapist–patient pair went on to meals, from meals to managing the household, then to managing her own body, then to interacting with immediate members of her family. But the journey took years and good apple pie makes the therapist smile, even to this day.

For the long treatment process, the family must have resources such as patience, time, and money. The treatment may be for the life of either the therapist or the patient. The treatment may also come to a mutually satisfactory conclusion when the thought disorder is not overtly manifested and the affective outcome is fairly well tolerated by the patient's family. There are special work conditions which support schizophrenic patients, and sometimes the patient is able to end the treatment when the work situation is stabilized.

To treat a schizophrenic patient using the technique of dynamic psychotherapy, the therapist must hold his own reality point of view in check and for a time share the patient's reality. Most importantly, the therapist needs to, minute by minute, move back and forth in his own mind between unreality and reality. He must decide, within minutes, whether or not to interject a reality point into the fabric of the patient's unreality. This particular ability on the part of the therapist requires that the therapist has a very comfortable relationship with his own unconscious. He must be knowledgeable about the overt manifestations of unconscious conflicts and have the courage to swim in the deep dark waters of unreality. Antipsychotic medication is helpful to insulate the unreality from aggressive intrusion into the reality of the therapeutic relationship. Frieda Fromm-Reichmann would understand.

Patients in the Mood Disorder Spectrum

Depressive disorders come with a wide variety of names. Some have genetic underpinnings and some do not. Major depressive disorder, psychotic depression,

depression with or without anxiety, and the bipolar disorders, are examples of illnesses with severe mood disturbance. Many clinicians argue that some of the depressive disorders are probably subsets of bipolar disorder. There may be overlap with some schizophrenic-like symptoms. In addition, mood disorders are often comorbid with other disorders and sometimes confused with other disorders.

Commonly, mood states vary widely in degree and kind. Mood is central to the human condition. Without the rich, complex mood states we experience, life would be felt as numbingly flat. Clinically, we are making a distinction between mood and emotion. Mood is an overarching feeling state—euphoria, awe, bright, neutral, flat, bleak, negative, and/or pessimistic. Emotions are more specific and focused, as in joy, grief, anger, hate, love, guilt, shame, and/or sadness. There is an overlap between emotion and mood. A given mood might be constituted by a combination of emotions. Joy, love, and/or pleasure could be thought of as ingredients for a "good mood." When the emotions are more negative and powerful such as shame, sadness, and/or anger, a "bad mood" follows. When our emotions are unregulated and conflict laden, the mood may be unstable, depressive, or euphoric.

Just as intense emotions can disrupt us, so can mood swings, chronic depression, or chronic hypomania. Patients with mood disorders are at significant risk for suicidal ideation, gestures, and attempts. Any clinician faces a severe challenge in treating them and to do so must be well-trained and updated regarding the latest clinical findings and research.

The psychodynamic psychotherapist should have considerable exposure to mood disorder training in an appropriate clinical environment. Diagnosis and treatment are major problems with a large percentage of mood disorder patients. For example, diagnostically, a patient with bipolar disorder may also have a general anxiety disorder, or an attention deficit disorder, or a borderline personality disorder. Sometimes a general disorder such as an anxiety disorder will constitute a breakdown in mood stability. It is not uncommon for severe anxiety to have a strong depressive component. The treatment can be frustrated by a variety of problems. Research has indicated that the presence of significant anxiety increases the risk of suicide. Failure to eliminate all symptoms to full remission increases the likelihood of relapse. In our experience, the noncompliance with medication among bipolar patients is quite high.

An effective therapist must decide whether his or her training in treating these disorders is extensive enough or not. If not, referrals out should be made. Treating depressive patients requires careful assessment of the nature of the depression, including such considerations as whether it is severe or mild, with or without anxiety. Is there some biological basis? Is substance abuse and/or comorbid personality disorder part of the clinical picture? The various possibilities make the task of determining a correct diagnosis more complicated.

Mike, a thirty-seven-year-old high-powered consultant, was a dynamic performer who made a great deal of money and excited customers and colleagues alike with his boundless energy and intelligence. His tendency toward outbursts of intense irritability and reactivity, however, seemed to be getting him into trouble for several years. He referred himself for a therapeutic interview after an incident in which he scared the living daylights out of a hapless colleague who happened to disagree with him on a work-related matter. That incident was one of several and underscored Mike's difficulty in staying focused on detail. Certain organizational and administrative tasks seemed beyond him.

During his first interview with the therapist, Mike talked intensely and nonstop about his work, his philosophy, his wife, and his plans for the future. Not only was the therapist unable to have a dialogue and raise questions, but by the end of the session the therapist was exhausted. When asked if this was his normal style, Mike looked up and said, "Yeah, people say I can get pretty wound up." At one point in the middle of one of Mike's monologues, in the same conversational tone, he mentioned his "special relationship" with three heads of foreign countries and his service as an adviser to the CIA. The therapist had a pretty good idea that Mike was manic and then discovered through further questioning that Mike also had some significant down periods when he felt "awful despair" and even some suicidal ideation. Mania combined with a dash of psychosis makes a challenging and sometimes dangerous patient.

The therapist chose to arrange for Mike to have an abbreviated psychological battery. The results were strongly supportive of a bipolar II disorder. Some indication of an attention deficit was also present. The therapist was uncertain about the attention deficit disorder but certain about the bipolar disorder. She then chose to refer Mike for medication and in coordination with the psychopharmacologist, agreed to try a medication that would modulate Mike's irritability and anger.

Medications are unavoidable with most bipolar disorders and many unipolar depressions. Finding the right medications can be a challenging process when there is no comorbid disorder. When there is one, the process becomes even more complicated. Any therapist working with these disorders must understand how to assess whether medications are helping and their side effects.

After a week, Mike presented for therapy looking and sounding much calmer. He reported feeling more at ease and less agitated both at work and at home. Furthermore, the question of attention deficit was resolved in that he also reported finishing a significant piece of detailed paperwork that he had always avoided. The medication was not one of those most commonly used. The therapist and psychiatrist felt that Mike's hypomania manifested itself as productive energy combined with the tendency for irritability and reactivity. Choosing to address these symptoms first, the split treatment team seemed to have been successful with the anticonvulsant gabapentin in treating the agitation generated by the hypomania. As the question of attention deficit fell to the background, they were then able to add an antidepressant to obtain a rather quick resolution of the medication problem.

The example of Cassie described earlier in the "adequate theoretical/conceptual frameworks" section is a good example of a difficult medication process. Finding the right meds and titrating them for Cassie took more than two years. When Cassie was first seen, her bipolar disorder was in a "rapid cycling" phase. That is, she could move from depressed to manic rather quickly—up to four times a week. This usually occurs in people whose condition began before they were seventeen years old and seems to slow down a few years after it begins. Rapid cycling is an illness course modifier, not a subtype diagnostically. People with rapid cycling tendencies could be bipolar I, II, or manic, mixed manic, or depressed.

During the two-year-period, Cassie's meds were changed dozens of times. Because Cassie was rapid cycling, and because she had high levels of anxiety, she was put on six different mood stabilizers at various dose levels and five different antidepressants in combination with the various mood stabilizers. In addition, she was put on three different benzodiazepines as well as buspirone for anxiety and on several sleep medications. For a long time each readjustment was followed by a problem. Sometimes she would react to a medication adjustment with the destabilization of her mood from mania to depression or vice versa. Many times the side effects were intolerable—sluggishness, jitteriness, nausea, and a host of other symptoms. Several times, after a reasonably good balance had been achieved, Cassie's weight changed significantly and seemed to affect the medications.

These two examples are a clear indication of the wide spectral range of such disorders. In one case, success was achieved fairly quickly. In the other, it took two years to reach a reasonable stable point so that further work titrating the meds and finding a maintenance level was possible. These are the kinds of circumstances that face any therapist who chooses to work with this patient population. There are more extreme examples of patients in the mood disorder spectrum who are delusional, homicidal, suicidal, and combative. They often end up in the hospital for a period of time, and then discharged for outpatient treatment once some measure of medication stabilization is achieved. The well-trained psychotherapist knows of these kinds of patients and makes choices about whether or not to treat them based on an extensive evaluation and on his or her training as well as the patient's interest in treatment.

Note

1. Hannah Green, *I Never Promised You a Rose Garden* (New York: Signet, 1964).

10

Disorders of the Borderline Syndrome

I can't see your face in my mind.

—Jim Morrison of The Doors

PERHAPS THE MOST TRYING OF ALL NONPSYCHOTIC DISORDERS are those considered part of a "borderline syndrome." If one listens to people who have lived with a patient with a borderline syndrome, one will hear disheartening stories of disturbed object relations. This kind of patient exemplifies the old adage "no good deed will go unpunished."

Summarizing, these people point out that when living with a borderline patient, one will tend to:

- Conceal thoughts and feelings because of the fear of the reaction and the certainty of the nasty fight that will follow.
- Feel like he/she is walking on eggshells much of the time and that any expressed feelings will be twisted and used against him/her.
- Feel blamed and criticized for everything wrong in the relationship, even when it makes no logical sense.
- Feel like there is always a problem or issue to contend with.
- Feel like the target for intense, even violent, irrational rages alternating with periods of perfectly normal and loving behavior.
- Feel manipulated, controlled, or even lied to at times.
- Experience the borderline person as a "Dr. Jekyll and Mr. Hyde": one moment loving and caring; another moment vicious and barely recognizable,

wondering which one is "real" and hoping that it's a phase that will go away—but it doesn't.

- Have a roller coaster relationship with high highs (things are incredible, fantastic) and very low lows (feeling of despair, depression, grief for the loss of the first relationship).
- Feel afraid to ask for things in the relationship because of the reaction—being seen as too demanding or being told one's needs are wrong or not important.
- See the borderline person act just fine in front of other people, so no one believes explanations about what's going on.
- Feel nothing is ever right, and that expectations are ever changing.
- The rules keep changing and no matter what, one can't win.
- Feel helpless and trapped.
- Experience being accused of doing things never done and of saying things never said.

The same list could apply to living with some alcoholics. What does a competent psychotherapist need to understand about such patients? The term "borderline" is unfortunately confusing. The term initially referred to what was previously understood to be a disparate collection of diagnostic entities such as "infantile personality," "unstable personality," "pseudo-neurotic schizophrenia," and "borderline schizophrenia" to name a few. A number of clinicians viewed some of these diagnoses as being in the affective disorder category while others thought of these diagnoses as being on the "borderline of psychosis." After the research peaked in the 1960s and 1970s, the term "borderline" had gained such widespread use that it was difficult to change (even though these patients are not psychotic). How can we make comprehensible the experience of life of a borderline patient? It is one of the most complex and confusing disorders known in mental health. The psychotherapist who wishes to work with such patients should be very familiar with the challenges and limitations of such work. Too many borderline patients in a practice may be hazardous to the mental health of the therapist.

Perhaps we should start with the term most frequently used by patients in therapy to describe that state of mind, that empty place they find in themselves. It is difficult to obtain unambiguous and revealing accounts of the tortured emotional experiences of the borderline patient. Nonetheless, we offer a glimpse into that terrible place some patients have called "the dead zone" by tapping into the accounts offered by patients who have been there. One patient wrote that she was "always scared and empty, like a void. Always feeling on edge. Will I always be like . . . this? I feel so all alone. No matter what, it's like I'm not real, not here, like the living dead; no, not even dead . . . just . . . nothing."[1]

As is often the case with complex personality disorders, many different descriptive accounts are given. Some patients reject the qualifier "dead" combined with "zone," preferring instead terms such as "intense conflict," or "nonzone." One patient found different metaphors more helpful as she rejected the dead zone imagery altogether. "It is not a zone, because to me that implies a place in which something is, an inexplicable oneness of being and peace. I am both the thing and the space and the time, and nothing comes in or out because there is no out or time or separateness. The snow metaphor seems more apt. It is a whiteout." And, as if to emphasize her objection to the term "dead," she added, "I wish it were the dead zone because in such a place one could be free of feeling—for that is to me what dead implies—but it is a place void of understanding."

Patients may describe their borderline experiences differently and they experience an inner world of feeling leading to contradictions in their behavior. They may distort and destroy their perspective and their relations with others and their sense of well-being. Emotional tidal waves known as *affect storms* may rage for hours or days, reappearing and then suddenly disappearing, leaving their most valued intimates exhausted, confused, and frustrated. Borderline behavior is a rule-by-chaos phenomenon. Borderline patients often cannot control their emotional state. Instead the emotional state controls them.

These patients vary in degree of severity and level of functioning. Briefly, the psychiatric manual (DSM-IV-TR) list the characteristics as follows: "Intense and chaotic efforts to escape the experience of deadness. A disturbance in identity formation or sense of self. An incapacity to maintain stable, intimate relationships."[2]

We find most borderline patients plowing through life tormented by chronic feelings of emptiness, intense loneliness, blankness, and numbness, as if living in a black hole. They often feel left on the edge of confusion, wracked by intolerable tension and consumed by alienation and desolation. Generally, borderline patients create chaos and disorder, as well as anger and despair in many if not most aspects of their personal lives. Shifting from one emotional state to another, they are often self-damaging, engaged in impulsive actions, and experience profound and consuming identity conflicts. When asked, they will attempt to justify themselves with a long list of rationalizations such as "I was angry," "I'm being mistreated," "I just wanted to have fun," "I am incensed at injustice," "I'm just a rebel," "I want to live life to the fullest," "I was feeling bored," "I'm just different, and the world can't handle it," and so on, as if these explanations were entirely acceptable excuses for their aberrant behaviors.

The essence of the disturbance is currently being clarified by clinical concepts emerging from psychoanalytic research such as splitting and object constancy. Hoping to avoid making our discussion too technical, we will refer to splitting as a weakness in a person's ability to integrate the different sides of him- or herself or different sides of others into one complex, whole personality. Poor object constancy is a psychologic condition that exists when the person is having great difficulty in mentally accessing her experiences with significant people (images or representations). This is what we think is behind the song title by singer Jim Morrison from The Doors of the late 1960s, "I can't see your face in my mind." That may be precisely why they feel so empty and desperately alone—and so would any of us under those conditions.

There are a number of movies we believe reflect various manifestations of the borderline disorders at different levels of severity. A few of them are *A Danger of Love* (1992), *After Hours* (1985), *Basic Instinct* (1992), *Betty Blue* (1986), *Fatal Attraction* (1987), *Frances* (1982), *Girl, Interrupted* (1999), *Looking for Mr. Goodbar* (1977), *Misery* (1990), *Play Misty for Me* (1971), *Single White Female* (1992), *The Rose* (1974), *The Doors* (1991), and *Gia* (1998).

The nettlesome nature of this disorder causes many clinicians to avoid treating them. Again, the competent psychotherapist knows her strengths and limitations. Don't treat too many at one time.

Notes

1. Gerald A. Faris and Ralph M. Faris, *Living in the Dead Zone: Janis Joplin and Jim Morrison: Understanding Borderline Personality Disorders* (Slade Books, 2001), 2–8.
2. American Psychiatric Association, *Diagnostic and Statistical Manual of Mental Disorders DSM-IV-TR Fourth Edition* (Text Revision, 2000).

11

Coordinated Split Treatment

Too many cooks spoil the porridge. Two heads are better than one.

By split treatment we mean a psychotherapeutic situation in which a psychiatrist manages a medication regimen and usually a non-physician therapist conducts the psychotherapy. Three or four decades ago, it was known as a T/A split and usually took place in an inpatient setting. The T was for therapist and the A was for administration. The T/A split was a medical model for what is called split treatment today. In the hospital setting the therapist might be a social worker, a psychologist, or a psychiatrist. The administrator might be a social worker, psychologist, or psychiatrist but usually a psychiatrist would be one-half of the split. In the hospital, everyone was paid by the month not by the hour, and there was always time to meet with the partner of the split. In those days almost every therapist had personal experience with psychotherapy themselves.

But with private practice there is very little financial incentive to meet with the partner in the split treatment. Without an ongoing dialogue about the patients that are shared in the split treatment model, that model can be subverted and the therapy might not go well, and neither would the administration of medication. The financial rewards for the physician to see four patients in the hour instead of one patient per hour are great since they are usually paid by the number of patients seen.

Disadvantages of Split Treatment

There are a number of disadvantages to split treatment and one very great benefit. The benefit is that another professional sees the patient and provides a second opinion and an objective view for the primary therapist to work with. Countertransference issues may be noted and worked with more quickly and freely for the therapy's progress.

The disadvantages are quite practical. In reality, the therapist and medication management specialist may not have the time or inclination to talk together. Moreover, the therapist may not even know the medication management psychiatrist. At this time prospective patients may call saying that their therapist told them to get a psychiatrist to give them "something." There may be little input from the therapist to the medicator regarding the signs and symptoms that suggest a need for medication even though the therapist probably knows the patient much better from their numerous psychotherapy sessions. A good-enough therapist is aware of this problem.

Yet, quite often the therapist refers someone for antidepressant, missing the underlying signs of a more disruptive, underlying, general anxiety disorder—a kind of free-floating, diffused feeling of uneasiness. If the medication specialist hasn't the time to fully evaluate the patient and the therapist doesn't fully communicate the patient's history and his experience of the patient in the sessions, the anxiety will not be taken into account and the treatment process will be ineffective. As psychotherapy training becomes a smaller fraction of the knowledge base, there is a tendency to follow the descriptive model of diagnoses rather than the explanatory psychodynamic model. That is, we adjust our therapeutic sights on behavior to the exclusion of thoughts and feelings.

Examples of the Problem

John, a thirty-four-year-old married father of two, had been to see two different therapists over a period of six years. The second one determined that John was an adult with an attention deficit disorder and a dysthymic disorder. John was given the stimulant Adderal and the antidepressant Welbutrin. After a year and a half John was only slightly improved. Eventually John consulted a third therapist. A careful evaluation revealed that despite his outward appearance of relative calm, John was suffering from a severe anxiety state. Overtly, his ability to mask this made him appear somewhat mellow while covertly he was hiding his feelings of agitation, irritability, and extreme nervousness. Thus his behavior led to the diagnosis of ADHD, but his feelings lead to the diagnosis of anxiety.

This information conveyed to the psychiatrist resulted in an adjustment to John's medications that ultimately proved effective. He was placed on an anxiolytic and something for sleep. After two weeks the disorganization and confusion that suggested attention deficit became less pronounced. His agitation and anxiety were dissipated. He was amazed and stated bluntly, "I never thought it was possible to feel this good on a daily basis." This is an example of a case where neither the therapist nor the psychiatrist had an adequate grasp of John's condition. The psychiatrist most likely could not take sufficient time to ferret out the underlying anxiety, and the therapist had little or no communication with the psychiatrist so that they were able to use each others' understanding of the case in order to treat the patient better.

Another instance of a problem in split treatment occurs when a therapist arranges for a patient to see a medication specialist, but doesn't know how to properly monitor progress. Many patients simply discontinue the meds if they have some side effect and never tell the therapist. Often the therapist doesn't even ask about the meds, assuming that the medicator is following the patient. Sometimes it is true and sometimes it is not true. An effective pharmacotherapist is in need of feedback from the psychotherapist and vice versa. In many cases feedback is less likely because the therapist and the medication management specialist may not have the time or inclination to talk together. Even more than that, the therapist may not even know the medication management specialist and not wish to spend the time or energy on a collaboration that is not financially rewarding or professionally gratifying.

Many psychiatrists follow the split treatment model today. Patients have come to expect to see a medication specialist and a psychotherapist. However, in some cases the medication may blunt certain emotions, that is, anger, irritability, uneasiness, and dissatisfaction. The therapist therefore may not see that the patient is not making progress through psychotherapeutic change. The psychiatrist may see the patient for a brief quarter-hour or less and will not have enough data to know whether the patient is improving or not. Sometimes the patient doesn't feel good taking a medication, discontinues it, and never returns to the medicator and/or the therapist. Thus, the treatment can fall apart in spite of the fact that both the psychotherapist and the pharmacotherapist are interested in continuing treatment and keeping the patient in a relatively "trouble-free" psychologic state.

Coordination Problems

Some split treatment situations involve complex contractual arrangements that in turn may result in a conflict of interest. When a psychotherapist treats an adolescent under the age of sixteen, she may not have any formal education to prepare her for the various organizational pulls that come from the school, the family, and sometimes the courts. One of the difficulties in treating psychological disorders is the tendency on the part of patients to not comply with the medication regimen. The system of split treatment fosters noncompliance, making it even more critical that the psychotherapist follow the patient very closely regarding his medication behavior.

Sally, a fifteen-year-old, was getting drunk every weekend. She "borrowed" the family car for her sixteen-year-old licensed driver boyfriend without the family's permission. The sixteen-year-old went through a stop sign and hit another car. Sally's school performance was poor. The school psychologist evaluated her and recommended consultation with the child psychiatrist, Dr. Smith, who depended on the school system for his referrals. The psychiatrist referred Sally to a social worker for psychotherapy, as well as to a psychopharmacologist. Both the psychopharmacologist and the social worker were dependent on Dr. Smith for their referrals. In fact, all three professionals shared an office and had a contractual business arrangement with the larger group of ten mental health professionals. The team leader and the CEO were the same person, Dr. Smith.

Psychotherapy was started, medication was begun. But Sally continued to drink, and her school and home functioning deteriorated. The child psychiatrist was consulted; the medication and the focus of psychotherapy were changed. The school was annoyed with Dr. Smith. The parents were exasperated, and Sally got into another automobile accident of a more serious nature. The sixteen-year-old boy was arrested. Sally went to live with a friend. Dr. Smith continued to receive school referrals. He has many managed-care contracts with HMOs. In some polls, HMOs have problematic reputations.

The contractual layers of this case prevented a better outcome. Dr. Smith wanted to please the school and the parents. He wanted the psychopharmacologist and a social worker to do what he thought was best for Sally. The social worker/psychotherapist wanted to please Dr. Smith, the parents, the school, and the psychopharmacologist. But the psychotherapist ought to have privileged the therapeutic relationship in an authentic way. A psychodynamic therapist must feel free to be empathic with Sally, not authoritative. We believe since there were so many unspoken business contracts involving Sally's therapy that the therapist was not free to honor the primary therapeutic contract with Sally.

Here is another example of poorly coordinated split treatment. The "medical model" is often used for a mental health group with a psychiatrist as the titular and professional head of the group. In every medical specialty, this model is more or less useful. In the fields where the technology is very difficult, e.g., eye surgery, a cadre of technical assistants ease the burden of the physician so that he can operate more effectively. In some fields, such as endocrinolgy, the physician has to puzzle the problem by himself.

The work of psychotherapy is technically more difficult than admitting or conducting medical tests and much more difficult than telling a patient what to do for a medical or surgical problem. The psychopharmacologist makes a contract with the patient to help evaluate and diagnose the psychiatric problem and then to help find the best medication with the least side effects to address the problem. But in the field of psychology, the subjective reactions of the patient may make assessment of the medications difficult. The pharmacologist tries to elicit enough information from the patient to offer the best psychopharmacologic advice.

Other Pitfalls in the System

The psychiatric patient is often not a good reporter, and the data needed to make the assessments may not be readily available from the patient in a fifteen-minute time frame. The pharmacotherapist may need to depend on data from the psychotherapist to make a well-informed decision regarding medication. But the pharmacotherapist and the psychotherapist do not bill the patient for their consultation time, so in practice, the pharmacotherapist does not get enough information. The two pitfalls in providing effective treatment revolve around the issue of data. The first pitfall is that the medicator can't get enough good data from the patient because of time constraints. The second pitfall is due to the likelihood that the communication with the consulting pharmacotherapist to inform him about their shared patient is inadequate. Both of these pitfalls occur in split treatments, but shouldn't. (They in fact can happen in any split treatment—psychiatric or medical.)

With the advent of the increased emphasis on proficiency in psychotherapy in the training of psychiatric residents, the physician might be able to extend the fifteen-minute medical management model. Then we have the phenomena of "poaching patients." The physician develops a positive countertransference to the patient and believes he can do a better job than the psychotherapist who already has an ongoing therapeutic relationship with the patient. The patient feels torn and herein lies the danger of split treatment. Thus, it is the patient who may get split—he may get worse, but usually interrupts treatment himself before serious harm occurs.

Integrated Split Treatment

Our experience suggests that split treatment can be done more effectively if the pharmacotherapy and the psychotherapy are conducted in an integrated manner. This means that the pharmacotherapist has to be quite skillful in addressing and assessing, within a limited data frame, how the psychotherapy might be impacting the neurophysiology of the patient's experience on the one hand, while the psychotherapist needs to be quite skillful in addressing and assessing how the medication may be impacting the psychotherapy experience of the patient on the other.

In any consideration of split treatment, it must be acknowledged that such treatment is easier than psychotherapy and psychopharmacotherapy at the same time. Since the focus of the two types of treatments are different, it makes sense to have them at separate times. It is easier to view the medication as something that is removed from the patient's responsibility. The medicating psychiatrist takes charge of what is not the patient's domain. But psychiatry is different from other medical specialties in that the patients often do not take the medications as prescribed. The patient believes that he can best manage his own psychotropic meds. Often the prescribing psychopharmacologist sees the patient just a few times a year and spends fifteen minutes with him. Patients usually do not offer enough information about their condition. A good pharmacologist would know what to do with that data if he could elicit it. A psychodynamic therapist should make sure the pharmacologist is regularly updated about the patient.

The diagnostic and statistical manual is a handbook that describes external behaviors, not a guide on interior states of feeling. Hopefully, the pharmacologist recognizes the indications of these interior states of feeling and works with the secondary derivatives of these states, that is, signs and symptoms. By working with the derivatives, a sense of authenticity in the therapeutic relationship, that is, "my doctor really understands me," does not develop. The patient's signs and symptoms are managed, but he may still feel he is the best person to judge his own feeling state and ought to have a great deal to say about how to manage his own medications. Of course, many patients are happy to have the doctor tell them what to do.

In split treatment, the patient is in a situation with two doctors or healing professionals that is similar to a child with divorced parents. The child is trying to play one professional against the other. Since the two professionals often do not communicate, the patient can succeed in splitting the treatment.

The psychopharmacologist makes a contract to prescribe medications, but as time goes by the doctor may get to know the patient and wonder why the patient isn't getting much better. The doctor may want to give advice that could run counter to the work of the therapist. A well-trained psychotherapist won't be giving much advice anyway, so the psychopharmacologist's advice becomes more powerful. The patient may feel caught in the middle between two authority figures. The treating psychotherapist will ask about the advice given by the psychopharmacologist and how the patient feels about it. A typical patient may cause a countertransference reaction in the prescribing physician. The patient calls a great many times. The complaint is that the medicine is causing too many side effects or is not working. The pharmacologist may get frustrated and shout "Did you ever think the problem might be you?" (This is a line that should make everyone chuckle. After all, this is psychiatry, psychology, and psychotherapy. If the patient weren't using projection as a defense mechanism, he would not need treatment!)

The listener psychotherapist may have an opinion about whether or not the patient will be able to work with a pharmacologist who isn't very tactful. In this field being right isn't always therapeutic.

Sometimes some patients such as those with borderline conditions and self-destructive tendencies are tormented by intolerable affects and need to project them onto the therapist and the pharmacologist. With this type of patient, frequent and sympathetic contact between the two health professionals is mandatory. If the patient does not improve over time, it may be necessary to reconsider the value of split treatment.

So clearly the pharmacotherapist and psychotherapist must communicate. They must sort out what is happening to the patient as the psychotherapy proceeds and as the medication takes effect. Pharmacotherapists working with insight-oriented psychotherapists must not ignore the internal shifts in the patient's state of mind as a result of the psychotherapy. The psychotherapist must be familiar enough with psychotropic medications to recognize when they may be enhancing and when they may be inhibiting therapeutic progress. Again, most importantly, they must be able and willing to communicate and work together. The view presented here indicating how split treatment should work will be difficult to implement without significant changes in attitudes and the way pharmacotherapists are paid. We fear that unless these issues are resolved, only those patients with sufficient monies will be able to receive (if they know how to insist) the integrated treatment that should be the standard.

III

THE NATURE OF THE CLINICAL EXPERIENCE

12

Patient–Therapist Motivations for Psychotherapy

> The uttered part of a man's life bears to the unuttered, unconscious part, a small unknown proportion.
>
> —Thomas Carlyle

MANY IF NOT MOST HUMAN MOTIVATIONS ARE COMPLEX, psychological, biologic, social, and mostly unconscious. We think of them as composed of overlapping layers of actions, thoughts, feelings, and beliefs. The therapist's beliefs are created out of personal fantasies, imagination, training, education, and the influence of the therapist's older, experienced supervisor. Education and supervision, therapeutic experience and personal beliefs are integrated into more complex therapeutic beliefs and generate a strong motivational force. The therapist must feel attached to the work of psychotherapy. Without that attachment, the work will not feel authentic to the patient nor to the therapist.

The theoretical model of treatment may vary somewhat within the larger frame of psychodynamic psychotherapy, but what the individual therapist believes will be more significant to the patient than the academic theory. A psychological attachment to the work makes it possible for the therapist to continue with the same patient over a considerable length of time. The durability of the treatment process allows a closer examination of the vicissitudes of the patient's psyche in response to the conflicts of everyday life. As the responses to everyday conflicts unfold, the unique character defenses that influence the patient's response to these conflicts are exposed. A good therapist would wonder how the patient developed his individual capacity to feel emotions and whether or not that capacity was functioning well or had become derailed.

Human beings generally have the minimally required character traits of curiosity, altruism, integrity, and commitment sufficient to allow for the formation of a therapeutic alliance. The needed sense of responsibility of providing a holding place for a patient's psyche throughout good times and bad can prove daunting for some therapists. When the therapist feels anxious and impatient, and fears to see a particular patient, the sense of responsibility may be insufficient to carry the work of the treatment and give the treatment process durability.

Certain beliefs are necessary to hold out hope for the patient. The patient walks in to the consultation room hoping that the therapist will make him feel better, that the therapist will provide answers to some confusing questions, and that the therapist will offer a feeling of reassurance that the patient is not going to drown in an ocean of psychological seaweed.

Therapist Motivations

The therapist, hopefully, is motivated by the belief that there is a chance the patient may improve with the professional interest and inquiry of a psychotherapeutic relationship. The therapist believes there is a special kind of talking the therapist offers that may be helpful to the patient. Emotions, thoughts, and behaviors are inextricably linked in ways that may or may not be obvious. The psychodynamic psychotherapist believes that she has a better understanding of these linkages than the patient and believes that she has the ability to work with these linkages in ways that will allow the patient to feel better.

Psychotherapists come from a variety of educations and with varying degrees of intelligence. Their motivations vary. There are psychotherapists who have college degrees in social work, psychology, nursing, and education. Some have master's degrees and doctoral degrees. Some have medical degrees. Some have left their original fields of law, engineering, and the humanities. Some have given up pediatrics or internal medicine to specialize in psychiatry. The psychodynamic psychotherapist may come from any of these backgrounds or disciplines.

A more salient question asks about the specific psychotherapy training and education of the individual. A good education may magnify a would-be therapist's motivation to be helpful psychotherapeutically. A poor education may serve to promote avoidance of a psychotherapy relationship. A critique of psychotherapy education is beyond the scope of this book. We believe that psychotherapy education depends on inpatient experience with a variety of patients, personal therapy and supervision, continuing education and a substantial number of clinical hours in an outpatient setting. A formal education involves extensive diagnostic work, technical work, endless reading, seminars, and studies of child development. Some experience with research is helpful. Some knowledge in the related fields of anthropology, sociology, genetics, and neuroscience is also helpful. A broad academic background will add to a therapist's education and sophistication. Education, personal psychotherapy, and of course extensive supervision are needed to enhance a therapist's motivation to do the work.

During the course of training, the therapist has incorporated and internalized certain attitudes of the training institution and the teachers. If the personal psychotherapy was important, the therapist in training will both emulate and discard some of the attributes and attitudes of her own therapist. The experience of working with different types of patients will influence the motivation of many therapists. Some therapists have little experience with psychotic, severe bipolar, or addictive patients and have little or no motivation for working with difficult patients. Many therapists will have experience treating borderline personality disordered patients but will not be interested in treating them. Others will be motivated by the challenge and the difficulty and may decide to treat borderline patients. Even so, the good-enough psychotherapist will recognize that she can only treat a limited number of borderline patients. She knows that the borderline patient's defenses and impulsive enactments cause a therapist a great deal of psychological strain. Nevertheless, the hope is that the borderline patient will get better and learn to function in a more ordinary way. The personal gratification for some therapists who can imagine success with borderline disorders may create a powerful motivation to engage in the treatment of them.

Toward the other end of the spectrum are those psychotherapists who do not want to work too hard, who do not want a regular job, and want to earn money without investing too much of themselves. The price of a psychotherapy education varies from inexpensive to very expensive. The price of the extensive personal supervision needed may be more than the price of the therapy hour for which the new therapist charges. Sometimes the therapist has lost a job with an institution and wants to be autonomous. Many are motivated by the wish to do work that pays and that suits a variety of needs. Some enjoy the social status that the work of psychotherapy brings. And others like the social relationship part of working with patients. Every patient has a unique story. We can be intrigued by the narrative and its unfolding. Some therapists like to talk and see psychotherapy as a chance to do just that with an attentive audience who pays for the privilege.

But the well-trained psychotherapist will sublimate the wish to earn money, the wish to talk, the wish for a social relationship, the wish to listen to a story, and the wish to rescue and impose beliefs on another person. Out of these sublimations will come a neutral kind of listening, an absence of the need to control another person, and a postponement of personal gratification. The sublimation capacity of the good-enough psychotherapist will be redirected to continual learning about the patient, teaching other therapists, perhaps some research, and the small pleasure of commitment, help, and accessibility.

Patient Motivations

"My wife wants a divorce." "I've been having panic attacks." "I feel very depressed a lot of the time." "My mother is making me crazy—it's always about her." "My husband is emotionally unavailable." "I wake up angry and go to sleep angry." "I don't need to be here—my parents think I do but I don't." "We are not getting along—he is irritable and critical much of the time." "I am in trouble at work—I've had some outbursts and I don't do my paperwork."

Patient motivations for seeking psychotherapy vary widely. The one thing they all have in common is misery. Very few show up and say "I am feeling very well and my life is going well but I thought it might be interesting just to learn something more about myself."

Sometimes the patient is clear about the reasons for coming and sometimes not. Problems with interpersonal relationships and family are among the most common. Painful feelings about the self are also common. Conflicted self-feelings that figure prominently in psychotherapy patients include a deep sense of inadequacy, narcissistic vulnerability, identity confusion, and fears of humiliation, to name a few. A significant number of people seek psychotherapy because they have been having major depressive episodes, manic episodes, anxiety attacks, paranoid ideas, or breaks with reality.

Patients want to find a way to take meaningful action that will enable them to return to normal functioning, find relief from a lifelong experience of misery, or resolve a problematic relationship. To do this they need to "put things together," fill in blanks in their thinking, take their coherent thoughts and determine what it is that prevents them from accomplishing meaningful action for change. The patient hopes that a good-enough psychotherapist can help, do magic, offer quick solutions, provide strategies for action.

Example 1: Interpersonal Issues as Motivation for Therapy

Here is a patient whose motive is partly created by his wife. Yet he too, in some vague way, may feel he has also contributed to the problem. So his motive for coming is of course to smooth over the conflict with his wife, and maybe, just maybe, understand himself better so as to acknowledge his part and accommodate his behavior. The therapist must see if that is so, that is, if indeed his motive includes a willingness to self-examine. He might be willing to be self-reflective, but the therapist must make it safe for him. Safe means that the exploration of the patient's contribution to his situation is not compromised by any anti-therapeutic motivations of the therapist.

Therapist: What brings you here?

Patient (Hank): I'm not sure why I am here. My wife wants me to come or she wants to separate.

Therapist: You're not sure why she feels that way?

Hank: Well, I don't know. She says something about me being abusive, negative, critical. Says I am impossible to live with anymore. But she is just unreasonable.

Therapist: What are you negative and critical about?

Hank: I don't know, I don't think I'm too critical. She just won't be reasonable.

Therapist: Can you give me an example?

Hank: Well, uh, all right, here's one. Just because I get after the kids to pick up after themselves, she says I am too critical. Their stuff is all over the place. I don't see anything wrong with getting them to be responsible. She gets all bent about it when I get on their case—says I am too harsh. With her too. Says I'm emotionally abusive to her and the kids. But how much can you stand? Their stuff is all over, they never do what they are told, never put anything away. (The patient is explaining his thinking, defending his view, and hoping for the therapist's support so as to calm his wife. He is not yet thinking that he might be at least part of the problem. His motives may include a not-yet-in-evidence need to accept some responsibility for the situation. If the patient's responses show motivation to fix things and his part in it, then the good-enough therapist, whose primary motive is the enjoyment of practicing a "let's figure it out" professionalism, can join with the patient and make the patient feel safe to do so. No lectures, no shaming, no intellectual posturing on the part of the therapist.)

Therapist: Uh huh. Do you think you are?

Hank: What?

Therapist: Emotionally abusive?

Hank: Well, that's what she says but how many times do I have to ask them to pick up their stuff?

Therapist: How old are your children?

Hank: We have a two-and-one-half-year-old and a four-year-old. (Here is where the therapist's motivations can interfere with or advance the therapy. If the therapist's motivations for this work include the desire to make linkages between thoughts, behaviors, and actions, then he will respond in ways that differ from a therapist whose motives are to feel narcissistically enhanced, who seek safe social engagements, or who are only interested in quick fixes.)

Therapist: (Raises eyebrows with facial expression that says with a hint of humor, "Hmmn, two-and-one-half and four? Gee!")

Hank: I know, I know, they are young but they can still do a little, can't they? (The patient has opened the door to further exploring his thoughts on the subject and it can be assumed that his motives do include a wish to come to terms with the issue. The therapist can now test the patient's motives more directly, unless the therapist feels enhanced when giving advice or is motivated only by money so that his training is inadequate. In such cases the therapist might become impatient and may lecture or perhaps discuss "behavioral strategies.")

Therapist: Well, some people might think they are a bit young to expect very much. Were you brought up that way? To be orderly and responsible at an early age?

Hank: Well, yeah. My father was a stickler for things like that. He used to say, "if you don't carry out your responsibilities around here, then you can go and not carry them out elsewhere." My mother would try to mediate but he ran the show.

Therapist: Are you saying that your dad was rather rigid about these things?

Hank: Yeah he was. Sometimes I was so angry I'd bang my head on the wall. (Here we see evidence of the patient himself having some strong feelings from his past that may serve to make him therapeutically responsive.)

Therapist: (silence).

Hank: So . . . maybe . . . maybe I can be a bit harsh. But my wife is too loose. (Here he acknowledges something about himself but tries to soften it by including his wife in the problem. But his motivation to resolve the problem at home seems to be real.)

Example 2: Family Issues as Motivation for Therapy

Therapist: What brings you here?

Patient (Gail): I am very depressed and agitated. My mother is making my life a hell. I'm forty-eight years old, have three teens at home, I work, and yet she expects me to be available whenever she wants. She ignores my kids—her own grandchildren. Never has a good word for me. Last autumn the *New York Times* ran a big interview on my work. I thought I had finally arrived. When I told her she said "oh" and "did I tell you about Janine's son pitching for the little league regional champs?" (This patient's motive for seeking therapy is not too difficult to fathom. She has been unable to come to terms with her mom's serious narcissistic personality. Still seeks the look of acceptance on the mother's face. The patient has been unwilling to give up hope and grieve for what was lost. Mothers are hard to give up on. The patient hopes that the therapist has some way of fixing it, of getting the longed-for connect with the mother.)

Example 3: Problems of Self-Feelings as Motivation for Therapy.

Therapist: So why are you here?

Patient (Mark): I have been feeling like hell lately . . . since I left my firm.

Therapist: What kind of work did you do?

Mark: I was a partner in an investment firm. We made a lot of money. But after twenty years my partners decided to change certain policies and directions that I wasn't comfortable with. So I left after a year of opposing the changes. I am only forty-eight. I can do anything I want but I can't get going. I don't feel right, not myself, don't have the confidence. I even had a panic attack last year. Thought it was a heart attack. Then the docs at the emergency room figured out that it was a panic attack. So they gave me some alpr . . . alprol?

Therapist: Alprazolam?

Mark: Yeah that's it. I've used it a couple of times in the past year. I can't believe I am having panic attacks. I have always been in control, always on top of things. (We see here this patient's immediate motive for seeking therapy is to cope with his panic attacks. However there is a deeper motive. He hints at it when he says "I don't feel right, not myself." It appears that something happened to him psychologically when he left his firm. He wants himself back as before. If on the one hand, the therapist is warm and supportive and aims to reassure by giving verbal support and encouragement, then we maintain that this is nothing more than hand-holding. If the therapist relies only on medication and support, the patient loses the chance to settle with his demons. The patient needs more than that. If the therapist's motive is to uncover what the underlying disruptive feelings are all about, then the therapy will be helpful. The therapist must stay neutral, professional, and exploratory, that is, "let's see if we can understand what might be happening to you.")

Therapist: Your panic attacks came on a while after you left the firm, is that correct?

Mark: Yes.

Therapist: Do you think there is a connection?

Mark: What do you mean?

Therapist: Well, you mentioned that you don't feel like yourself. That you are not confident anymore. Is it possible that something of who you are, that is your identity was compromised when you left the firm because you have invested such a large part of you in it?

Mark: (The patient pauses, stares at the therapist for some seconds. Then his head begins to nod in agreement.) Yeah, yeah. I put so much of myself into the firm for twenty years. I felt weird walking out the door and like I have been in a trance ever since. Yeah you're right. Jesus! (The patient now begins to think about himself and who he is now that he is no longer with the firm. He knows that leaving caused him some grief. However, he is not aware of how entrenched the problem has become. The patient's background set him up to "be somebody" only to the extent that he was productive. His family was not supportive; in fact his only escape from the anxiety of a chaotic family was to demonstrate his academic competence and diligence. Thus he was set up to, as an adult, form a basic identity based on productivity. The firm that he loved so much was the supporting and loving family he never had. When he left, he reverted back to the anxious, weakly defined self he once was as a child. Hence the panic attacks. This patient's work in therapy will be about expanding and firming his sense of himself and identity formation. It will take longer than he initially anticipates.)

In cases where the therapist is seeing a patient in a conflicted marriage, there is a tendency for some therapists to openly or unwittingly take a position as to outcome. If on the one hand, a therapist's motive is to keep people together regardless of the apparent wishes of one patient, then the therapist's bias about marriage is directing the outcome. Or if a therapist decides a patient should split and pushes for that, then again the therapist's bias is determining outcome. This isn't often good-enough psychotherapy.

We have seen couples who divorced because the therapist decided it was completely the other spouse's fault without hearing both sides. In our view, patients more typically must explore their own contributions and make decisions from a more self-aware place. We have seen couples who remained together not because they worked things out and chose to do so but because the therapist was personally resistant to divorce and pushed the couple to remain married.

When an outcome is pushed based on the biases and beliefs of the therapist, the therapist is making assumptions about the reliability of the patient's perceptions and reports. Consequently, the therapy doesn't fully explore (if at all) the patient's own contribution to the problem because the therapist's agenda and narcissism are in charge. (One exception to this might be when a patient or any children are at risk for physical injury. Then a therapist might need to act to protect.)

We have attempted to show through these few examples, how the motivations of both patient and therapist are woven together in an intricate process. The psychodynamic psychotherapist's motives must be driven by the desire to explore and reveal the hidden dimensions of the patient's motives, to uncover and to comprehend with and for the patient.

13

Empathy and Therapeutic Tact

Compassion is not enough

SYMPATHY, PITY, AND EMPATHY ARE HIGHLY SUBJECTIVE and may or may not be received in the way the therapist meant. We believe that sympathy and pity need to be used when socially appropriate, although we cannot imagine when it would be absolutely necessary. It might be nice, but not absolutely necessary. Empathy might be absolutely necessary and therapeutic. Clearly, empathy requires imagining what another person might feel under a particular set of circumstances. The therapist must be able to step out of her own shoes and step into someone else's for a few minutes at some point in the therapy hour. And this sense of empathy will be unconsciously conveyed by the therapist to the patient (mostly by non-verbal means) and will offer understanding and hope.

A belief, from a therapist's viewpoint, is created out of a collection of thoughts, feelings, and actions, which are synthesized into a strong motivational force. A therapist needs a set of beliefs in order to remain attached to the work of psychotherapy. The attachment to the work makes it possible for the therapist to continue with the same patient for an extended period of time. The therapist can then examine the vicissitudes of the patient's psyche in response to the conflicts of everyday life and the unique character defenses that influence the patient's response to those conflicts.

A sense of empathy is also necessary in order to develop therapeutic tact in a relationship. Therapeutic tact is a verbal intervention that encompasses empathy, interest, understanding, and neutrality. Such an intervention may be a clarifying question or an interpretation of a thought, feeling, or behavior.

Therapeutic tact is needed to help the patient understand why his seemingly coherent thought is not leading to meaningful action. Therapeutic tact can make it easier for the patient to give up his unreasonable, infantile wishes and replace them with realistic, reasonable, and adaptive ambitions.

A sense of empathy is helpful for the therapist to develop a tactful response to a patient. Empathy contributes to the therapist's understanding of the patient. When the therapist finds himself devoid of empathy, he probably doesn't understand the patient well enough to be tactful. A lack of tact may be interpreted by the patient as a lack of sympathy, understanding, or interest. The patient may translate a lack of understanding to a sense of not feeling safe in the therapeutic environment. Without a sense of safety, the patient may not be able to trust the therapist and may choose to walk away from the therapy situation.

Sympathy, pity, and empathy are human emotions that many or may not have a significant place in the therapist's repertoire. Therapeutic tact is a technical skill that should always have a significant position in the repertoire of the good-enough psychotherapist. The combination of neutrality and empathy will help the therapist develop tact.

If the therapist asks a clarifying question from a neutral point of view, then the patient will not feel put on the spot and the therapeutic alliance will have a chance to strengthen. For example, a therapist might say, "What was that experience like for you?" Many therapists might say, "was that experience hard for you to handle?" This second style may be heard as sympathetic but it might also be heard as the therapist thinking the patient wasn't up to handling the experience. Even though the supposition of the second question might be correct, it may not be therapeutically tactful. We think that if the question were asked tactfully and in an open-ended or neutral way, then the patient would be able to respond without feeling judged or criticized. It is a subtle difference.

A psychological evaluation is much easier when the patient feels that the therapist is approaching him from a tactful position. A tactful position helps the patient to believe that the therapist has the patient's best interest in mind. If the therapist is burdened by unconscious hostile wishes toward the patient, then the therapist may not be able to develop the necessary therapeutic tact with that particular patient. Sometimes these unconscious thoughts and fantasies may be expressed in various countertransference enactments that may be detrimental to the therapeutic alliance. The patient may translate the therapist's unconscious impulses internally as an assault on the patient's sense of self. Ultimately, the value of empathy and therapeutic tact is that they let patients feel safe enough to reflect on themselves without fear of disapproval.

14

How the Therapist's Mind Works

A different way of looking at things.

Given an authentic, competent psychotherapist, the next question, perhaps the most difficult to answer, is "how does a therapist's mind work?" What is the process going on in the therapist's mind while listening and observing, clarifying and questioning, challenging and interpreting? Can we really describe the workings of a good-enough therapist's mind in any meaningful way? We will try, though in the end we may only provide a glimpse.

Let's begin with some of the things good-enough psychotherapists do not do. Good-enough psychotherapists do not "wing it." They do not operate on whim; they do not take "wild shots" about the meaning of the patient's actions, moods, or feelings. They do not use mechanical methods and do not impose perfectionistic, narrow, or parochial standards. That is, they must be open-minded.

What effective therapists must do is have a foundation of fully elaborated and consciously held concepts, theories, and empirical databases derived from the clinical literature and from experience. In other words, the therapist must have a scaffolding. The scaffolding permits a therapist to engage fruitfully and objectively in the process of inquiry and hypothesis formation. Eventually the scaffolding is unconsciously and automatically employed. We have described that scaffolding in other chapters. How it is used depends on the artistry and creativity of the therapist. But before we discuss how artistry, creativity, tacit knowledge, and intuition are employed, we can describe the more easily recognized actions and attitudes of a competent psychodynamic therapist.

The central role of the kind of therapist we are talking about is that of a fearless and resourceful explorer, discoverer, or detective whose sole aim is to accompany the patient on a journey to understand the meaning of the patient's conflicts. To do this the therapist adopts certain attitudes that are designed to facilitate the journey.

The concept of psychological determinism holds that mental events have causes in the same way that physical events have causes. Almost everything the patient does or says may eventually be placed in some context that reveals another aspect of hidden conflict. In other words, just about every action, reaction, behavior, and attitude has some meaning. Sometimes a cigar is just a cigar, but not often. Silence means something, verbosity means something, intensity means something (anxiety, anger, agitation?), taking things too seriously or not seriously enough, means something, argumentativeness means something. The more pertinent question for the good-enough psychotherapist is, when is meaning therapeutically worth figuring out.

Another conscious attitude of the well-trained psychotherapist is the *principle of multiple function* (Robert Wälder).[1] A patient's behavior is more often than not the result of more than one underlying and mostly unconscious motive. A pathologically overweight woman may be overeating for any and all of the following reasons—self-nurturing as a result of a non-nurturing mother, soothing her feeling of loneliness in the world, maintaining her physical size to calm her unconscious fears of sexual assault, as well as to hold on to an unconscious identification with the mother of very early childhood. There may be other motivations as well. Any therapist hoping to work with such a patient successfully must realize when a patient's signs, symptoms, and feelings are overdetermined. The principle of multiple function works in step with overdetermination to allow the patient to use a given behavior as a defense, a wish, and/or a mechanism to advance the organization of the self.

A good psychodynamic therapist listens with an open mind and with what has been called "evenly hovering attention." The therapist observes, listens, questions, and clarifies as part of a process of data collection. Some therapists are taught the technique of listening for up to three-fourths of the session before making any observation or asking any question. Often this is pretty good idea. The creative therapist knows when the circumstances call for waiting or intervention. With some patients, silent but active listening is the best approach much of the time. For others it is unhelpful and counterproductive because they need a more verbally active therapist. It is a judgment call on the part of the good-enough therapist based on the patient's personality and the nature of the patient's inner conflict.

What does the good-enough therapist listen for? The therapist listens for the content of the patient's verbalizations and for missing content as well. He listens for affects, strong and weak, open and hidden. He listens for the tone and emotional quality of what the patient says. He listens for incongruity or mendacity. He listens for defensive maneuvers such as projection, avoidance, rationalization, and the tip-of-the-iceberg cues of hidden feelings and thoughts. One patient is always apologizing for real and imagined little irrelevancies. Another tries to organize the session by taking notes and asking for instructions on what to do between sessions. A third is always making small talk. And a fourth uses mostly passive verbs and describes feelings of having no options. In the active listening process of the good-enough therapist, mental notes are made for future reference. Not all verbalizations are useful. Some are just background noise.

To an outside observer much of what is being said in any given session might be seen as boring or unproductive. But the good-enough therapist knows how to evaluate the significance of small talk on the part of the patient as well as no talk, loquaciousness, intense talk, or vacuous talk.

What does the therapist try to observe? The talking cure is not just talk. Non-verbal cues of the patient's inner world such as body language, manner of dress, facial expressions, eye movement, eye contact, and expressions of surprise are noted by the therapist. One patient smiles constantly because she is nervous, another smiles not at all for the same reason. One patient offers good eye contact, another maintains an aggressive eye contact, and a third offers practically no eye contact.

A male patient's face reflects disdain for the whole idea of psychotherapy even though he referred himself because of panic attacks. His disdain defends him against feelings of humiliation. An adolescent brought in by her parents for acting out behaviors stares blankly at the therapist. The good-enough therapist knows enough to not remain silent too long with such a patient and also knows that most adolescents who are sullenly silent may not answer "yes" to an observation made by the therapist even if they agree with it. But they will answer with a strong "no" to an observation if they disagree with it. So the competent therapist will not be fooled by a sullen teenager's non-verbal behavior, but will advise the patient that not responding means yes because "I know that if I say anything you disagree with you won't let me get away with it and you will say no."

All the things a therapist listens for and watches for are part of an emotional/psychological puzzle. The pieces, once properly fit together, offer a way of comprehending the nature of the patient's conflicts. However, the therapist must be open-minded and not force fit pieces of the puzzle together and construct explanations of the material the patient provides before adequately examining the pieces.

What does the psychodynamic therapist do during data collection besides watching and listening? Well, he/she attends to patient reactions elicited by the therapist's own interventions or comments, questions for clarification, observations, and interpretations. A patient, after a diatribe against some criticism his wife leveled at him, notices the therapist has raised an eyebrow, or has shifted in the seat indicating surprise, a question, or increased interest. The patient stops and waits or maybe if he tends toward directness may ask the therapist, "What?" The therapist may be testing a small hypothesis. Is this patient able to reflect on his own contribution to his troubles? The therapist can be creative if he also is mindful of the discussion on empathy and therapeutic tact as described in the previous section. By using an incredulous tone regarding the patient's reaction to the wife, the therapist will learn how well the patient can engage his reflective functioning. "Do you feel that the level of your anger at her is justified by her criticism? Her comment doesn't even sound critical based on the way you mimicked her."

The hypothesis being tested is important. If the patient can acknowledge that he tends to overreact to things, then the therapist can go on questioning some of the behaviors he reports and the emotional roots of his overreacting. If on the other hand the patient repeatedly rejects the therapist's probing in this area and insists that he doesn't have much patience for all that psychobabble, or if he simply doesn't respond to the probe, then perhaps we have a different situation. Attorneys might call the gathering of information by checking out hypotheses, noting reactions, and verbal as well as non-verbal cues "discovery." But it is not done blindly.

As we stated earlier, the psychodynamic therapist has a scaffolding. The small hypotheses tested are derived from the scaffolding. In the example of the patient's diatribe about his wife, the therapist was obtaining a measure of "psychological mindedness," that is, can the patient come to recognize how much his developmental history influences his current behavior? Concepts such as psychological mindedness and the effects of childhood experiences are part of a necessary and intricately crafted scaffolding.

When the therapist feels enough material has been gathered from straightforward questions as well as the testing of small hypotheses, then maybe a new set of questions emerge. Who or what in the patient's background left him so vulnerable to angry outbursts? Is he angry only at the person closest to him or at others? Is he angry only with women or with men too? Is this behavior derived as a reaction to mom's interaction with him as a child? Or has he identified with an angry, harsh father so that he mistreats his wife the way his father mistreated his mother? The scaffolding helps to point us in the right direction if we are skillful enough to evolve the right hypotheses from the scaffolding.

Let's say that in the above example, the patient reports that his mother was a "saint" and was very nurturing and caring. And let's say that he remembers his father as good to him, but demeaning and emotionally abusive to mom. Further, the patient, when asked, readily accepts that he has the father's "get-up-and-go" attitude, runs a small business as the father did, and is well thought of in the community, as was the father. Now the therapist is perhaps wondering about the concept (from the scaffolding) of a strong paternal identification. The hypothesis, mostly unconscious in the mind of the therapist, may be stated as follows. Based on the patient's sense of himself as having many of his fathers characteristics, is it possible that he also manifests in his relationship with his wife, the same tendency to be dismissive and demeaning as his father had toward his mother?

To test this hypothesis, the therapist will need more information about how the patient feels about each parent and about the way his dad treated his mom. When questioned about this he reveals a deep affection for his mother, a deep respect blended with fear of his father. Then as he recounts his father's tone and behavior toward his mother, he suddenly becomes choked up and there are barely noticeable tears in his eyes. The patient then recalls how pained he felt about his mother's misery because of the father's harshness. At the same time he found it difficult to be critical of his father. How would a good-enough therapist think about this?

This man reported that he sought therapy because his wife had had enough of his harshness and demeaning behavior toward her. The therapist cannot know in any absolute way how to view the relationship between two people when only one is present. As a matter of good technique in general, a therapist should only examine the patient's behavior and how he copes with any situation involving anyone else. In this case the therapist did not need to know whether or not the patient's wife was in fact difficult. The therapist needed to consider the patient's responses to his wife in terms of reasonableness. Were there better ways to react than his over the top intensity? Based on the patient's description of events, did he create more conflict in the relationship? Were there other, underlying reasons for his reaction, that is, was he dissatisfied with his wife for other, unidentified reasons? When did he become so angry at his wife—before marriage, soon after marriage, after the children were born?

Assume that the patient reports that his agitation with his wife has been going on for six or seven years. He then recalls on questioning that he always loved her, but three or four years into their marriage, began feeling irritated with her over trivial things. A first child was born in the second year of marriage. So now let's describe the therapist's thinking and the formation of a new hypothesis derived from the scaffolding and based on the material so far.

The therapist's thinking is informed by training, which was quite conscious in the learning and supervision states but when applied in the clinical hour becomes unconscious and automatic. What does the therapist do with the data? Often a central disorganizing conflict is recognized—that is, just what underlying drives and defenses might be present to explain the patient's struggle? An awareness of the patient's particular traits of personality help explain some of the patient's style of response. An assessment of defenses is made, that is, what are the unconscious tactics by which the person contains disruptive thoughts and feelings to keep them out of awareness—rationalizing, avoiding, suppressing, repressing, idealizing and so on. Finally, the therapist must evaluate the possibility that a biological underpinning is involved in the patient's struggle.

The therapist ponders the material. No biological underpinning seems evident. What might be considered a central disorganizing conflict? Well, the patient loves his mother (and wife, too). Loves his father but is pained by memories of his father's harshness toward her. So maybe he brings to his marriage (from principles derived from the scaffolding) the same mix of action tendencies and reaction tendencies formed early in life from his experiences in the family. A boy needs to admire the father in order to feel good about himself. We see this at work when kids argue and one says, "My father can beat up your father." So the boy is going to adopt much of the father's ways, some consciously, most unconsciously, through a process called internalization. Defensively, the man continued to idealize the father to maintain his own self-worth. He also tended to use rationalizing to explain away the contradictions in his behavior rather than become aware of the painful effects associated with the father's abuse of the mother.

In addition, the therapist might think back to the scaffolding again and realize that children tend to instigate feelings in the parents, good and bad, stemming from the parent's own childhood experiences. Children after all do grow up and as adults tend to "reprise the conditions of childhood either in imitation or renunciation."

Based on education, training, experience, and intuition, the therapist might form a new, broader hypothesis and again for emphasis, apply it with therapeutic tact. Perhaps the patient became more agitated with his wife after she became a mother. Only after she became a mother would he be unconsciously stimulated into reprising his unresolved conflicts from childhood—a strong identification with his dad on the one side and the pain and sadness and love for his mother on the other. The patient became short-tempered and irritable with his wife because of a strong identification with his father. He automatically responded to her when she became a mother in the same periodically angry way his father did with his mother. One can appreciate the irony in the situation of a man who hated the way his father treated his mother, doing the same to his wife and exposing his children to the same sadness he experienced for the same reasons. But the scaffolding informs the therapist about how to think of the data gathered.

By framing the observation/interpretation of the material with "let's see if we can figure out how come this happens," the good-enough therapist has placed the patient's behavior in a context that takes pejorative attitudes and labels off the table. The message is "let us try to understand how these circumstances have come about" rather than blaming, shaming, moralizing, or persecuting. A good-enough psychotherapist conveys to the patient a dynamic psychotherapy perspective, directly and indirectly.

Some therapists are explicit about how therapy proceeds. For example, they might say something like this: "This form of psychotherapy is based on the idea that human behavior is driven by mostly unconscious motivations. The goal is to understand what these motivations are, what things mean, how have they come about. The answers are not that one is evil or stupid or weak or lazy or unmotivated in the larger sense. The world of the mind operates on the basis of cause and effect just as the physical world does. When a person says he doesn't know why he does some of the things he does or feels the way he feels, it doesn't mean there is no reason. So if you choose to pursue this therapy, we will be working on how the actions and attitudes and beliefs and emotions causing you trouble have come to be what they are."

So to continue with this case the therapist has formed a tentative hypothesis and proceeds to test it. A thought is offered to the patient: "You hated it when your dad mistreated your mom. I wonder if you have noticed if your children are upset when you're being somewhat like your dad by being very angry with their mother?" The patient will react to this. Perhaps he will recognize and react to the irony with a sense of shock. Maybe he will ask how this could happen. Maybe he will note the irony and reflect on it quietly and sadly. If he responds with either of these possibilities or something else that fits, then the therapist might draw upon the scaffolding again to frame a follow-up observation: "You may be like your dad in some ways you are not happy about."

If the patient agrees then another "interpretation" might be called for. An interpretation tries to tie things together with a proposed explanation for the material under discussion: "You seem to have joined with your dad as boys do to have his acceptance while feeling terrible about how he treated your mother. He became so much a part of you through the natural tendency for a boy to identify with a father that when you find yourself to be a father too, you act reflexively, like him sometimes—good to your children and harsh with your wife once she became a mother." The patient's reactions to this interpretation and others that follow will guide the therapist in building on the hypotheses or altering and refining them.

Once the therapist has considered the material and burnished it in the furnace of a questioning mind, and useful hypotheses have been formed and confirmed and interpretations made, the patient may slowly come to feel differently. As the great developmental psychologist and analyst, Erik Erikson wrote, all therapy can offer a patient "is a different way of looking at things." If a psychotherapist is successful, this new way of looking at things will be more than enough. One must be humble about these things. To paraphrase a colleague, life was going on long before psychotherapy came along.

The artistry, creativity, and intuitiveness of the "authentic," psychodynamic psychotherapist, using the scaffolding of empirical science is a patient's best hope for success.

Note

1. Robert Wälder, "The Principle of Multiple Function: Observations on Over Determination," *Psychoanalytic Quarterly* 5 (1936): 45–62.

15

Cognitive Style and the Therapeutic Alliance

Better to reign in hell than serve in heaven.

—John Milton, *Paradise Lost*

ONE OF THE MOST COMMON, RELENTLESS PERSONALITY TRAITS in the world is recognizable in the all-too-human reaction of Lucifer who was cast out of heaven for his oppositional attitudes and desire for autonomy. Such attitudes are found in all human personalities to some degree. There are those who are quite comfortable being compliant and accommodating and others who react intensely to the feeling of being controlled in any way. In toddlers we hear, "No, I want the grape posigle (popsicle) not the green posigle." In adolescents we hear, "It's my homework and my grades, let me do it when I want to." In adults we get the bill of rights—"I'll worship the way I want"; "You can't come in to my house unless I let you"; "You can't take my gun away." Autonomy is a big deal. Lucifer was asserting his dramatic, personal, human need for autonomy.

Obviously, an oversensitivity to being influenced is commonly seen in clinical practice and can be a problem to the extent that the patient experiences the therapist as someone who could exercise unwanted control. The psychodynamic psychotherapist is aware of and trained to manage this and the other attitudes and traits that arise from personality styles. The reality is that we can only treat the patient who walks in the door.

A patient's personality/cognitive style inevitably influences the development of the therapeutic alliance. The well-trained psychotherapist must be minimally defended and very self-aware to work effectively in a dyadic situation with these cognitive styles. One style or another may be difficult for the therapist for different reasons. Just imagine the therapist with a tendency toward passivity coping with a patient with a passive style. The useful mental energy in those therapy sessions might be underwhelming! An overview of styles and how they may impact the therapeutic relationship will be helpful.

A patient's personality or psychological style, for the purposes of this book, means the characteristic, relatively enduring way he/she thinks, pays attention, experiences, and remembers interactions with other people and the environment. Some might call this "cognitive style." It is not the same as "learning style" but cognitive style may include learning style. Another way of thinking of our personality or cognitive styles is that they refer to the way individuals vary in their perceptions, reasoning, remembering, and experience of life. We will use the terms "personality style," "cognitive style," and "psychological style" interchangeably. Psychodynamic clinicians think of these styles as on a continuum of variation from typical to disordered.

Even "normal" personality styles can create difficulty in the therapeutic process. If a patient's style is connected with intense, unregulated affect and if a therapist does not have a well-regulated and modulated affective system of his/her own, then the personality/cognitive style might cause the therapist to develop a sense of frustration. An overview of some common styles and how they may impact the therapeutic relationship will be helpful here.

Some Common Styles

The Self-Referential Style

The *self-referential style* is recognizable because the patient uses himself as a standard to judge other people. Often his personal standard is set quite high because he cannot tolerate disappointment in himself and so he cannot tolerate disappointment in others, including his therapist. Such a self-referential style may also be recognized as narcissistic or self-centered. When someone in a group tells an anecdote, the self-referential person will inevitably respond with some anecdote where he was the center of attention. So in a psychotherapy situation, this patient is so pleased to be the center of attention that he quickly becomes emotionally attached to the therapist and the therapist may feel that the patient is too close. This patient wants to go to the same doctor, the same restaurant, and the same concert as the therapist. The therapist may want to go away on a long vacation and not return.

Another type of self-referential patient is only too aware that he wants too much attention. He may then have a depressive reaction in defense against his wanting too much attention. The defense unconsciously goes like this: "No one wants me; I have no friends." In adolescents we may hear "my friends all hate me."

The transference paradigm involves the patient thinking that the therapist is only there because the patient is paying. When the reality of things and fantasy, defense and resistance all find a common pathway with the therapeutic alliance, it may be difficult to tease the strands apart. The patient usually regards the reality case to be most compelling and may influence the therapist to think that way also. The competent psychotherapist will avoid this conscious pitfall—since the nature of the work is that every patient pays a fee. Instead the focus of attention should be on the defense and the concomitant "no one wants me." If the therapist falls into the reality trap of reassurance, "oh there must be people in the world that find you appealing," we would point out that if the patient believed the obvious reality, he wouldn't be sitting in the office. So we would submit that the appropriate therapeutic response is "that's a lousy spot to be in, isn't it?"

This latter response means that the good-enough psychotherapist has imagined what it would be like if he were in the social and emotional position that the patient believed himself to be in. The therapist must override, set aside, or store in a library of the brain for future reference the reality complaints of the patient. By setting aside the complaints, the therapist can lighten the emotional position the reality complaints force on the patient. The therapist might now be able to forge a therapeutic alliance whether or not the patient is compliant. All the patient has to do is show up, pay the bill, and not be too socially inappropriate, that is, he can't hit the therapist or break the office furniture.

The Suspicious Style

The *suspicious style* is recognizable in the patient who manifests a tendency toward pervasive distrust and suspiciousness of others and tends to interpret the motives of others as questionable at minimum. The assumption is that others are more likely to exploit or deceive. Patients are often bothered by doubts about the loyalty of others and find it hard to forgive injuries. They commonly see others as manipulative. People with this suspicious style have a righteous sense of self and think of themselves as always at risk for being mistreated by others. They are prepared to "fight the good fight" because they are certainly right and others are wrong.

Such patients struggle with subsurface feelings of anger, resentment, hostility, and overwhelming fear. These suspicious style patients, when trying to cope with such poorly understood, weakly integrated feelings as intense anxiety and hostility, tend to automatically extend their style to contain these feelings. For example, the therapist might find these patients disowning their unfavorable traits, being rigid in considering observations by the therapist, and quite vulnerable to stress or unexpected change. Many of these patients are prone to conflict with authority figures, attempt to exert their own "push back power" against people in authority, and have difficulty with supervisors. They tend to provoke hostility in others and can give "hair trigger" responses to trivial behavior from others.

Given this kind of cognitive style one can see how, in order to defend against the feelings of threat (of humiliation or exploitation), these patients may be unable to form the necessary therapeutic alliance with the therapist. In their perceived need to protect themselves one can recognize in them varying degrees of tension, abrasive irritability, arrogance, interpersonal antagonism, hypersensitivity, cautiousness, self-righteousness resistance to external influence, and an inclination to be contentious and litigious.

With such a cognitive style of rigid, hostile defenses the therapy can be stalemated or interrupted and countertransference feelings will usually develop in most therapists. Thus the patient's cognitive style of caution may be useful in the real world, but in the psychotherapy world its use is overextended to contain the feelings of threatened exploitation and humiliation, and therefore may stymie the therapeutic process. We can also see that in the suspicious patient, elements of self-referential thinking are present. So again, style is just that—it is not a scientific category.

A competent psychotherapist must know, among other things, that it will not do to be too confrontational with this patient or for the therapist to appear to have a strong investment in the ideas and observations shared with the patient. In fact, the therapist's attitude might give the patient the idea that the therapist has a little or no great personal investment in the thoughts that are shared with the patient, that they are hypotheses that will be easily discarded if not validated. So a flexibly benign attitude of nonchalance is used.

A good-enough psychotherapist will not debate or argue with a mistrustful patient who is misinterpreting some situation. Rather than be caught up in debating the pros and cons of a patient's distortion of reality, the good-enough therapist might simply ask, "Are there other ways to explain the situation?" or "Can you imagine alternatives to your view of the situation?" Humor may be useful but never at their expense. Noting the irony in situations, comments of a philosophical nature, and a steady lack of personal investment in moving the therapy in any particular direction is essential.

The suspicious style interferes with the formation of the therapeutic alliance because the persistence of the suspiciousness and the rigid, hostile defenses call for a high order of creativity in technique. Again as we have said, therapists whose emotional state is insufficiently regulated and moderated will not respond well to these patient cognitive styles and will find it difficult to be creative in technique. In the case of a suspicious patient, countertransference feelings of anxiety and hostility may arise in the therapist, paralleling some of the patient's feelings. The therapist may begin to experience the patient as mean and nasty as in Thomas Paine's comment that "suspicion is the companion of mean souls and the bane of all good society."[1] Any chance for a therapeutic alliance can be lost under such circumstances and a stalemate will develop and the patient leaves treatment.

The Rational/Objective Style

The *rational/objective* style is to be recognized by the patient's heavy reliance on reason and logic. There is a pattern of preoccupation with structure and control at the expense of flexibility and efficiency and a strong emphasis on responsibility. They tend to see others as too casual, irresponsible, self-indulgent, or incompetent and have intense, conflicting feelings toward both themselves and others.

The rational/objective patient prefers polite, correct personal relationships. They relate to others in terms of rank or status and in general can be inconsiderate and dominating, with a strong adherence to authority and moral causes, and an overvaluation of good form and logic. It is this kind of patient that makes one think of the old aphorism "logic is a means of arriving at the wrong conclusion with absolute certainty." Patients with this style are usually deferential to authority but can be quite autocratic and condemnatory with subordinates. Challenged to support their position they will justify their insensitive or aggressive behavior by recourse to rules or authorities higher than themselves.

Rational/objective patients keep most emotions under tight control. Emotional experiences for many of these patients tend to be solemn, tense, and grim. These cognitive style patients are harshly self-critical, restrain their own feelings, and neglect themselves emotionally. They can experience severe internal conflicts, especially in personal relationships, and it seems as though the more they adjust to the wishes of others, the more they feel anger and resentment. Such patients may be exasperating to deal with. They have difficulty making decisions with a characteristic air of austerity and serious-mindedness. It is this type of person for whom the question "are we having fun yet?" was raised.

Rational/objective patients have their own system of rules, of shoulds and oughts. They like their ducks lined up, overvalue predictability, and have a general dislike for surprises. Unpredictable events are not well received because in being unanticipated, they upset the idea of being in control. The lack of a feeling of being in control, of having had all the bases covered, is an anxiety-ridden experience. Thus such patients tend to live in the future, that is, they plan and ruminate about anticipating all possible outcomes in order to avoid vague, unidentified dangers.

These personality styles employ their well-developed analytical capacities to rationalize their actions as based on objective assessments, actions unconsciously driven by a need to find safety from poorly integrated anxieties about being humiliated or proven imperfect. To maintain their stability against the upsurge of poorly organized, fearful affects they will expand their cognitive style characteristics and over-intellectualize, quoting higher, intangible-philosophical points of view. Emotions may be isolated from conscious consideration and oppositional attitudes taken against their own impulses.

These patients often seek treatment because their productivity is slipping. They may be depressed and feel unable to maintain their normal level of functioning. They frequently experience psychosomatic disorders because of a tendency to stifle internal tensions. Many rational style patients may experience severe anxiety, panic attacks, sexual impotence, and exhaustion. These patients are not well enough attuned to the reactions and the feelings of others. Often such patients seek treatment because of someone else's complaints about their behavior—for example, people who are tired of the obstinacy, controlling attitudes, and contentiousness or poor job performance reviews as a result of personal problems getting along with other workers.

Initially rational style patients appear to be cooperative. They are polite, unemotional, logical, and detail-oriented. They will want to defer to the therapist and be good patients. Serious, conscientious, and honest, they will present as motivated and hardworking. In time, however, they tend to be overtly cooperative and covertly (but unconsciously) oppositional. Their conflicts with compliance and defiance will appear in the therapeutic alliance soon enough.

Rational style patients then, can be stubborn and can appear quite imperturbable, refusing to be deflected from their own convictions and purposes. The well-trained, good-enough psychotherapist will not be drawn into intellectual diversions and the superficial compliance and instead stay focused on patients' unacknowledged affects and conflicts. A good-enough psychotherapist might find these kinds of patients frustrating and difficult to work with because of their contentiousness with words, their readiness to split hairs, their attempts to make trivial changes in the therapist's observations and to resist exploration of feeling states.

The Impressionistic Style

The *impressionistic style* is recognizable by features such as vagueness, exaggerated expression of strong and sometimes shallow thoughts and feelings, a reactive pattern of labile emotionality and a lively, dramatic enthusiasm. (We tend to think of this style as more common to women, but it is probably just as common in men but may look slightly different.) This style is far less likely to use logical analysis because the person is powerfully influenced by emotions, at times to the exclusion of a reality and facts. Unlike the cautious style patients who tend to rationalize and selectively interpret facts, these patients pay little attention to facts. Their perceptual/cognitive impressionism gives rise to the obverse of the old saying, which might apply to cautious style patients, "they can't see the woods for the trees." Instead, the impressionistic style patients "can't see the trees for the woods." It seems that they have a dislike for annoying detail, just the opposite of cautious style patients who can't ignore detail.

Impressionistic style patients tend to be more extroverted than introverted. Extroversion involves the tendency to be outgoing, talkative, convivial, warm and affectionate, energetic, and vigorous. In a non-pathological form, extroversion is being high-spirited, buoyant, and optimistic. These factors can constitute a personality disorder only when the needs and emotions behind the behavior are pathologically inflexible, repetitious, and unintegrated. Persistent exploitation of others (including the therapist) can develop and the personality disordered version of the impressionistic style becomes apparent.

Overly impressionistic/global style patients are more likely to be somewhat emotionally immature, dramatic, and shallow, the more global and impressionistic, the more dramatic and shallow. Both men and women of this style tend to engage in uninhibited behavior. Such women might display affective labiality and manipulativeness. They might engage in intense but brief relationships. In such men, uninhibited behavior may be demonstrated through neurotic internal conflicts, impulsivity, aggressive behavior, drug abuse, interpersonal exploitation, and numerous shallow, sexual relationships.

In the area of close relationships, emotions may be pitted against reason. The heart rules the head. The emotions speak at times without listening to the voice of reason. When at work, most people can put their emotions on the side and use their capacity to reason, to use their intellect. But at home in a love relationship, they succumb to the power of emotion. The attention they focus on others does not necessarily help them to a better understanding of others. Their intense observations of personal relationships are aimed at discerning what behaviors, attitudes, or feelings are most likely to result in obtaining the emotional support and approval they seek. They are acutely aware of other people's attention. The point is to gauge how they are being seen and accepted by others and as a result they tend to be easily influenced by others.

Many of these patients think of themselves in relationships as much closer or more significant than they really are to the other person. They often do not see when they are being ignored or humored by others who have become tired of their exaggerated emotional style.

Impressionistic patients favor the emotional side of their nature and bring that style not only to love relationships but also to interactions with people they don't know well. At the mild end of the continuum, the person may appear outgoing, genial, friendly, and fun loving. At the more extreme end of the continuum they may not be well understood in the workplace. They may become depressed when their emotional style has resulted in disappointment rather than feelings of joy and pleasure. These patients can get very angry. Others will not understand the depth of their anger, and for the most part neither will the patient. Therapists often called these angry outbursts "a blast from the past." In such circumstances, patients have had an emotional reaction fueled by a previous disappointment that they were helpless to repair. When a present time occurrence reminds these patients unconsciously of the previous disappointment, we suggest that the emotional response has been multiplied by the number of historic years since the original event.

Usually, the more extreme impressionistic patients are harder to treat. But studying the clinical literature about them can be helpful in demonstrating certain psychotherapeutic techniques. Since the emotions are so much on the surface, the patient will form a hopeful attachment to the therapist rather quickly. If the therapist is interested in the emotional reactions of these patients, they will feel that interest as a good thing. These patients will not be disappointed, at least not initially. However, if the therapist becomes more interested in the patient's relationships rather than in the emotions those relationships stir up, the patient will gradually feel disappointment in the therapist. The treatment may start to stalemate and the therapist will not understand where the therapy went off-track. The patient will be sent for a psychopharmacological consult and a round of medications will begin. The patient will become more frustrated and may stop the medication merry-go-round and drop out of treatment. The therapist will call the patient non-compliant. The therapeutic alliance founders on a technical error of avoiding the patient's affects.

Note

1. Thomas Paine, *Common Sense* (New York: Dover Publications, 1997), 41.

16

Addressing the Patient's Need to Fight

Man is sometimes extraordinarily, passionately, in love with suffering.

—Dostoevski

We think Dostoevski was on to something. Sometimes patients need to fight the therapist. We humans, perhaps in the interest of personal emotional security, seem to prefer "the devil we know than the devil we don't know." Or is it better stated that the typical human tendency is to stay with the self-defeating pattern we are familiar with than face the unknown demons underlying the pattern?

The psychodynamic psychotherapist must have a sense of this element of patient behavior. In order to understand patients who need to fight with the therapist, it will be necessary to speculate on underlying conflicts residing in the patient's unconscious. We can build a speculative theory of the case and then offer interventions that are based on those speculations.

Conflict with a therapist usually makes most patients uncomfortable. Most patients avoid fighting with their therapists because of their dependence on the therapist for improvement in their mental health. The patient chooses what to say in the consultation room, as does the therapist. When a patient chooses to say something provocative to the therapist, when a patient chooses to cancel the next regular appointment, when a patient is late without sufficient reason, when the patient takes the psychotropic medication in a contradictory fashion, the patient may be fighting with the therapist.

Pieces of action that are not verbalized are called "enactments." Ambivalent feelings may be the underpinning of many enactments. Enactments are often disguised ways for the patient to fight with the therapist. Sometimes the good-enough therapist may choose to interpret the ambivalence. At other times good clinical judgment will require the postponement of a quick foray into the realm of ambivalence until further clarification about the particular issue evolves. Ambivalence, enactment, and unconscious aggression are associated with a patient's need to fight with the therapist.

Mrs. Burns came to the first session complaining that she felt weak in her relationships with her husband and children. She felt strongest at work and was able to manage quite independently there. She cried and was fearful that her adolescent children did not love her. She was concerned that her husband belittled her in front of the children. She refused to go out socially with other people because he humiliated her in public. The therapist agreed to meet with her once weekly and postponed the use of medication until her symptoms were clarified.

After several sessions where Mrs. Burns repeatedly asked the therapist to tell her what to do, the therapist remarked that if she would talk about her feelings, after a while it would become clear to her about what to do and she would not need to be told. She was annoyed with the therapist at that but remained polite. She then canceled the following session. The therapist wasn't surprised.

The next time Mrs. Burns was seen the therapist had internally decided to take up the issue that dependence sometimes makes a person feel weak. Then the person would believe she was weak and might act weak and her children might be having a hard time with that. The sessions continued and every now and then the therapist would make an interpretation that followed the above theory of the case. One day the patient said she didn't like coming to therapy because she was worried that it meant she was weak and that's what her husband said. That was followed with, "but I like you."

The therapist suggested that when Mrs. Burns lost her temper in front of the children, she looks and feels out of control. "A weak person is out of control." She began to manage her angry outbursts at home and seemed much less concerned about being weak. When Mother's Day came, her children offered loving and admiring messages and she felt gratified. And her husband continued to humiliate her but she now will stand up to him and tell him how she feels.

At the end of six months, the patient felt much stronger, no longer cried, felt happier with herself. She remained married to a man who believes himself to be very smart, capable, important, and loving. She stopped treatment when she felt stronger, when she felt like an important parent and was resigned to being smarter in relation to an ego-centered man.

This is, from our point of view, a good outcome for half a year of psychotherapy. This effective psychotherapist thought that Mrs. Burns had fought with her, initially, but had not felt belittled in the therapy sessions and so put up with the therapist.

Patients may be anxious discussing information about themselves but that resistance is usually conscious and readily explained to the patient's satisfaction. However, when the patient believes that the therapist would use private information as a way of controlling her, she'll become anxious in the therapy session and may use displacement to disguise the issue. The patient will talk about someone at work who was trying to find out about some personal material. If this is a new complaint, it most likely is a transference issue being displaced onto someone at work. We see the displacement as a resistance to the treatment process and a sign that the patient is ambivalent about the therapy but too polite to engage in an overt fight with the therapist. This is perhaps one of the more subtle elements of the psychotherapy process and depends on the experience and training of the good-enough psychotherapist to interpret the displaced fight.

A transference paradigm that involves suspiciousness should make the psychotherapist wish to inquire into early childhood psychological issues. The psychotherapist might suspect that the child had experiences where she was not permitted to pursue her developmental milestones in an appropriate way. She may have perceived her parents as being suffocating and over-controlling. This doesn't mean that her parents were in fact over-controlling but rather the patient's elaboration of her childhood experience amplified her parental internal structures as being intrusive. So should it surprise a good-enough psychotherapist that such a patient would fight with her therapist?

17

The Place of Dreams in the Therapeutic Process

> The dream is theater where the dreamer is at once scene, actor, prompter, stage manager, author, audience, and critic.
>
> —William Shakespeare

WHAT IS A DREAM? Why do humans dream? How do we understand a dream? Dreams have been part of the human experience at least as long as there have been Homo sapiens. The ancients thought of dreams as part of the supernatural world. Consider Joseph and his coat of many colors, sold into slavery by jealous brothers and then rose up to become an adviser and interpreter of the dreams of the Pharaoh. The Greeks also believed in the divine origin of dreams. Both the Egyptians and the Greeks sought help for troubled lives and circumstances by interpreting dreams through priests in the temples.

Heraclitus, Plato, and Aristotle eventually came to regard dreams as something coming from the mind of the person. They rejected the idea that dreams were messages from the gods. Some modern, biological reviewers consider dreams the by-product of neurological activity, mental flotsam composed of leftover fragments of thoughts and feelings the person experienced during awake time. However, the new research in neuro-psychology and memory supports the analytic assertion that dreams have meaning and are a reflection of the dreamer's own life. Dreams take place through specific, complex neural pathways and involve many aspects of brain functioning including the motivation centers of the brain. A good-enough therapist should recognize through training and clinical experience that the patient's dreams reflect the concerns, fears, interests, and mixed moods that are present when the patient is awake either consciously or unconsciously.

Dreams are interesting sleep phenomena which are usually forgotten during the day. Dreams show the dreamer a different perspective than the one from his everyday life. That perspective may at times excite the dreamer or frighten him or puzzle him. The dreamer may notice that the feeling in the dream is not necessarily connected in any logical way to the action in the dream. When the dreamer awakens, he may remember the disconnect and may wish to make sense of the dream.

In telling the dream to his therapist, the dreamer's hope is that some sense will be made of the dream and the dreamer will then have a deeper understanding of himself. The dreamer is gratified if the therapist shows interest in the dream. We would expect the good-enough therapist to be trained and learned in the way to use dream work for the benefit of the patient.

Some patients do not remember their dreams and report other kinds of things that have more common reference points, such as movies, plays, or books. But once a psychotherapy patient reports feelings about a movie, the therapist may hear it as though it might be a dream. The therapist might ask, what was the most touching thing or what seemed most familiar or what was scary about the movie? The therapist might be looking for some kind of metaphor or irony or paradox. Maybe the dreamer will report an uncomfortable emotion or a powerful wish. It often seems that the patient borrows the work of the artist, who wrote the play or book, as a vehicle to say something about himself. In this regard, reported dreams, books, or films may corroborate what the therapist had been thinking about the patient. A reported dream may help move the therapy into previously avoided areas.

The story of Anna will demonstrate how the threads of dream work, transference, and countertransference can help the good-enough therapist shed light on a painful tragedy.

In the fourth hour after Anna's beginning psychotherapy at a once-weekly frequency, she reported the following dream: "I was in the park at the pond feeding the ducks with my son Tommy when he was four years old. We were having such a good time, the two of us. We did that a lot. He was such a nice boy."

The patient's associations to the dream concerned the boy's suicide and his accomplishments in his high school. Anna talked about how difficult it would be to go to his graduation. The principal had called asking her to come to the graduation to receive Tommy's diploma. Anna said, "Everyone says I should be strong, that I have to continue with my life."

Therapist: What is it about the graduation that is especially difficult?

Anna: I don't want to be the object of pity—the mother of a suicide. I miss him so.

Therapist: The graduation can be very impersonal.

Anna: Yes, it's too awful. I can go to other things that memorialize him. My husband doesn't want to go. But I have to be strong.

Therapist: I don't know that you have to be strong. Sometimes when we lose someone we love very much, we don't want to be pitied.

During this exchange, the therapist was thinking that suicide must be one of the most awful experiences for the person who is left alive. The patient's dream showed that she wanted her son restored to her as he was before he became severely depressed. The therapist remembered that when we lose someone, we feel ashamed. When the parent punishes a child by removing a privilege, the child feels shame and the social justice system starts to work.

But to be an object of pity was a shameful thing for Anna. The issue is not strength but shame—an emotion that is almost impossible to bear when tied to guilt. Anna felt guilty that she had not been a good parent. She felt public shame that she was the mother of a suicide and she felt the tragic loss of her single child who chose to leave her in this tragic way.

The above material was very difficult to listen to without resorting to defensive platitudes such as "remember the good times in the park" and "now you have to be strong." These are the statements that friends and family make but a therapist must interpret the pain in order to help ease it. The therapist's last statement was such an interpretation.

The night after the reported hour, the therapist has an empathic dream. The therapist dreams that her grandson is crying and her daughter-in-law doesn't want the baby to be picked up. The therapist looked at the baby in the crib saying "nice boy, nice boy." In reality, however, the therapist's daughter-in-law always wants the baby to be picked up when he is crying, so the dream structure was about not being able to hold the grandson. The words "nice boy," of course, borrowed the patient's words and incorporated them into the countertransference dream. This was an unusual dream for the therapist and allowed her to get in touch with Anna's longing for the lost boy that would be referenced appropriately in the many hours to come. It was the complex reaction of a very sharp psychotherapist.

At other times, the dream or the book or the movie may be used as a way to avoid talking about an immediate real-life conflict. When the hour becomes burdened with too many details and begins to use up too much time, the dreamer may want to entertain himself and/or his therapist with a wonderful narrative. So the dream can be offered as a means of moving the therapy process forward or a way of holding the treatment back. It will be a wise psychotherapist who can distinguish between the two situations and who will know how to proceed in either direction.

Many psychotherapists are not trained to help a patient understand his dreams and often do not ask for dreams. A patient may not offer them as an interesting view into his mind.

Dreams are useful adjuncts in helping the patient understand his own development. The young man who draws a beautiful bridge on paper and then dreams of an intricate set of suspension cables is one version of a castle in the air. To make the dream a reality, the young man will have to go to engineering school and learn mechanical drawing and some sophisticated mathematics. If he feels that his dream can never develop into reality, he might be too ambitious or he might be inhibited or he might be depressed. Maybe his math skills are woefully inadequate, maybe his father said he was stupid, or maybe he identified with an ineffective parent. This dream can be viewed as a wish and may also be a solution to a problem. The good-enough therapist can help the patient understand the separation between the dream and the reality and offer him the potential to achieve his developmental task, that is, the ability to work.

Another type of dream related to the development of a human being is common among pregnant women and expectant fathers. The parents may dream that the unborn baby is out of the womb and walking and talking and looking just like somebody. Here the parent has taken the dream step of nurturing the unborn infant into a young toddler who walks and talks. The pleasure parents feel when they remember this type of dream helps them face the reality of no sleep and no time for themselves when that little person finally comes into the world. When the expectant parent has an anxiety dream related to the infant, the therapist is in a privileged position to help the patient understand his anxiety and perhaps make some suggestions that might alleviate those uncomfortable feelings. The therapist has then worked toward helping the patient achieve a developmental milestone of good parenting. Not a trivial intervention in today's world.

Dreams may provide clues concerning the family dynamics of the patient. Such dreams may involve the parent or a parent substitute or a stranger with a set of characteristics similar to a parent. These dreams may be quite complex and cause the patient to avoid talking about the psychological issues that are exposed. Sometimes such dreams may be an overt representation of a piece of family history.

Mary dreamed she went to see her mother and her mother shut the door in her face. Such a dream may also represent anticipated fear but it will likely open the hour up to discuss Mary's conflicts with her mother. But this is the kind of dream that the patient may not want to remember or the therapist may not be trained to understand. So it may never come into the therapy hour, especially if the therapist doesn't periodically ask about dreams. Perhaps Mary really wants to shut the door in her mother's face but she lacks the courage. Perhaps Mary believes that her mother has been an intrusive parent and would rather have had a different mother. Mary's grandmother may have been an important maternal figure and may have superseded Mary's mother. So Mary may be struggling with the guilt generated by that particular family dynamic. The effective therapist is obliged to imagine different possibilities and try to bring to the surface the intervention that will move the therapeutic process forward.

18

Psychopharmacology and the Complexity of Psychodynamics

Therapist 1: You will need antidepressants for the rest of your life.
Therapist 2: You need to sort some things out, not medication.

THE DRUG ARMAMENTARIUM IN THE HANDS OF PSYCHIATRISTS TODAY is truly extraordinary. There are psychotropic drugs for just about everything—anxiety, panic, low mood, low-energy, too much energy, problems with concentration, sleep difficulties, agitation, irritation, confused thinking, aggressive tendencies, suicidal tendencies, and many more. And of course meds make it unnecessary for the therapist to work so hard. Therapists don't have to know so much, they get paid anyway. Creativity is less important to a therapist who relies on meds to relieve symptoms and may have no interest in pursuing the patient's psychodynamics.

Psychotropic medications and psychodynamic psychotherapy intersect in widely different ways, depending on the patient's characteristics. One size does not fit all patients. By this we mean that patients who are more educated tend to be more patient in pursuing psychological resolution. It does seem to us that education does teach patience. The healthiest people, relatively speaking, are more likely to seek exploratory psychotherapy. The question of when to use psychotropic meds with children and adolescents is still being researched.

If, on the other hand, a patient is not greatly interested in listening to the melody of his or her mind and more interested in excitement, that is another story. They may wish to be left alone. They may wish to establish that nothing is wrong. They may wish to not work hard. They may wish not to be bothered. The yearning for these things is powerful. The wish becomes a reality.

Regarding these patients we can only say, go ahead and wish upon a star but don't be a sore loser.

The effective psychotherapist must, of necessity, be aware that common psychotropic meds have specific applications and various side effects. This does not mean that the therapist should become a medicator. It means that in order to collaborate in a coordinated split treatment relationship with a psychiatrist or a psychopharmacologist, the competent psychotherapist must be able to monitor the benefits and unhelpful side effects a patient may be experiencing from a medication regimen. The therapist will most likely see the patient weekly, but the medicator only monthly in the beginning, even less after awhile. So the therapist must be alert to the impact of the medication and realistically review progress and the patient's expectations of relief.

Having made this point however, we now feel the need to address the more complicated relationship between medication and psychotherapy. There are two important aspects of this relationship to be emphasized.

First, we believe that it is more difficult to determine whether or not a patient needs medication than is commonly assumed in clinical practice. The intricate, subtle, confusing, and hidden elements of the human mind are not so readily understood. Some therapists would immediately recommend medication for a patient who presents as depressed and who does not describe a particularly stressful current life circumstance. In such cases, however, we would point out that many factors of childhood and adolescence as well as personality are at play in all of us. Therefore, we would expect a competent psychotherapist to conduct a thorough review of an individual's childhood history, sense of self, pattern of object relations, and conditions of daily life before recommending medication for depression.

A strong family history of major depression is certainly an important consideration for medication. But the situation is not simple. Even people from families with genetic predisposition for depression or any mood disorder should not be automatically considered biologically vulnerable just because they seem to present with any mood disorder bipolar symptoms. A psychodynamic therapist knows how children can identify with a depressed parent or a bipolar parent without themselves having the biological vulnerability. Furthermore, some people who may not appear to need medications may periodically have outbreaks of quasi-psychotic thinking and actions such as manic episodes or major depressive episodes. In between they may well appear to be perfectly fine. The themes of their melodies are not so easy to discern.

Second, medications can be troublesome to the therapeutic process when for example, SSRIs such as Prozac, Zoloft, or Lexapro cause the patient to feel cognitively and emotionally blunted, as if his brain were wrapped in cotton. The patient may only be vaguely aware of this "blunting." But an alert therapist might well notice it. In some cases, patients whose presenting symptoms have been greatly alleviated by the implementation of psychotropic meds sometimes lose interest in resolving the underlying conflicts that created the symptoms in the first place. Their anxiety may have been reduced below optimum level to maintain motivation for exploring their inner world. It is also difficult to identify the effects of medication on the person's perceptions and on how affects have been altered so as to confound the therapeutic process.

Examples of Patients and Meds

Meds have their place. But we would like to give a few examples of how easy it is for problems to crop up around the interaction of meds and therapy.

Example 1

Joanne had seen two therapists before seeking a consultation with a third after five years of treatment with the second therapist. She was diagnosed as having a major depression and was told she would be on antidepressants for the rest of her life. She had improved somewhat in the five-year treatment but was dissatisfied because she still felt pessimistic, unhappy, harried, and ignored. She continued to have periodic panic attacks for which she was given an anxiolytic.

Joanne was forty-two, a mother of three who worked full-time in a good job where she made twice as much money as her husband. They had married young, both of them in order to escape from very unhappy homes. Over the course of the twenty-two-year marriage, Joanne's husband had become more and more detached and less and less a father to his children. This was similar to his own upbringing.

Joanne's family of origin included three sisters and two brothers, a quiet, nonresponsive father, and a religiously fanatical mother. The mother expected Joanne to conform to a rigid religious dogma. She was disdainful of Joanne and treated her more like a hired hand instead of a daughter. Joanne never argued with her mother or asserted any of her own thoughts and feelings. Over the years the relationship had continued to be conflicted and discouraging for Joanne. Her mother did not come to her wedding, or to the hospital when her grandchildren were born, or to their birthday celebrations. Nothing Joanne did ever changed her mother's silent rejection of this one of four daughters. Joanne feared further rejection by her mother if she deviated from the mother's rigid expectations.

The third therapist reviewed the material presented and worked with Joanne in four exploratory/evaluative sessions. It became apparent that Joanne, like so many women, found it next to impossible to give up on the hope for a loving relationship with her mother. The despair one finds in women who feel their mothers have not accepted or valued them or allowed dissent and/or disagreement from early on, is profound. Even when a good-enough therapist does proceed to explore a mother–daughter relationship that has failed from early childhood, the reaction of many if not most women patients in this state of affairs is to experience a "daughter's fog." There is a loss of intellectual and emotional focus when discussing the relationship and the outcome is that these patients appear mesmerized.

The third therapist recognized the external conflicts that involved a detached and financially irresponsible husband and a need to help her unhappy children. The despair over the early childhood failure of the mother–daughter relationship that had affected her whole life created the internal conflicts. After working with her for eighteen months, she was able to work through her grief and longing for maternal response. She no longer feared her mother's disapproval of her for divorcing. Joanne realized that her expectation for acceptance by mother was futile and that her own sense of self was sufficient to move her life forward.

This common, deeply felt need by a daughter for acceptance by the mother seems to endure without letup unless something like psychotherapy makes it possible to work it through. Even if Mom did respond to Joanne as hoped for, it would not change anything. The story of the red balloon is appropriate to this situation between mother and daughter. A three-year-old child is taken to a parade by her parents. She wishes to have a red balloon sold at these parades but her parents cannot afford it. So year after year she is disappointed. Finally when she is twelve years old she has accumulated some money from her paper route. When the next parade takes place she immediately runs over to the balloon salesman and buys one. After a few minutes she lets it go up in the air—a red balloon simply is not experienced by a twelve-year-old in the way it would have been experienced by a three-or four-year-old. And neither would acceptance responses by her mother do for Joanne now what they would have done in early childhood. An adult can't experience such feelings the way a child would.

Slowly Joanne's dark, despairing mood lifted. She confronted her husband about the circumstances, and because of his intransigence and lack of psychological mindedness, she initiated divorce proceedings. And finally before the end of six months she was completely off medications. The therapist received phone calls four years later. Joanne had remarried and was very happy with her new husband. The therapist, after about two months, realized that medications had been used instead of the psychodynamic psychotherapy that Joanne needed to resolve what were emotional conflicts. Sorting out the interwoven strands between psychodynamics and psychopharmacology is a requisite for a good-enough psychotherapist.

Joanne's life was affected by the relationship with mom early on and in a way that should be understood by psychodynamic clinicians. As a further explanation, it can be noted that some women patients react with what one of us (GAF) calls "daughter fog," a peculiar feeling of being "spaced out" when discussing early childhood relationships with their mothers. Psychologically, mothers and daughters do appear to be permanently tied at the hip. The other (RB) considers such a state to be a "preverbal blur" and offers the following perspective on a fascinating area of child development—an expanded explanation useful for psychodynamic psychotherapists.

The newborn's smile changes rather quickly from reflexive and reactive to social/interpersonal, in a matter of weeks. When a parent leaves and a stranger enters, the well-developed smile disappears and apprehension, dismay, fear, and tears may follow in seconds. The infant has a cry that the parent tries to interpret but there are no real words for communication. Language comes to the child in the first years of life. Organized memories that bear some resemblance to historical truth come even later.

Through these early developmental years, the parent–child duo must try to communicate with one another so that the child reaches her normal developmental milestones. In this early era when language is rudimentary and limited, impressions and emotions are stored in a very young child's mind. But complex words are not attached to these complex sensations that impact the child in a variety of ways. The child cannot explain and learn what's going on. The parent guesses. The parent believes she's guessing right. But she's probably guessing right only most of the time. Thankfully, the baby appreciates that the parent will try to adjust the guess when the baby continues to cry.

But meanwhile, the emotional meter keeps on ticking. The infant is trying to get fed when hungry, get changed when wet, and get rocked when unhappy. There are no words as of yet. This era gets stored in the infant's memory in intricate neurological processes but is reflected clinically in the older child, adolescent, and adult as a pre-verbal blur. Because this history and intricate data set is not available in the consultation room, the clinician is forced to speculate and guess about the emotions and impressions of the patient sitting in the opposite chair. Of course the patient can only guess as well.

There will be times in the treatment process in which both clinician and patient seem to fall back into a reverie, a reverie reminiscent of the early era of the preverbal blur. An emotion that interrupts, an enactment not easily understood, a distortion of reality are some examples of small, rather mild regressions to a more primitive psychological time before the patient had words. Sometimes the patient uses body language (for example, a shrug) or stereotypic words like "whatever" or "I guess," to indicate to the clinician that the patient is avoiding an unconscious melody of emotion that has regressive and preverbal meaning. These small regressions are significant in the treatment process. They point to places that should be tactfully explored when the time is appropriate.

If these small melodies of psychological slips or regressions are explored prematurely, the patient will feel assaulted, intruded upon, and left without defenses or understanding. The therapist will have made the patient feel bad. Many therapists are all too aware of this clinical dilemma. They may avoid the dilemma altogether so that the patient feels progress has not been made. The treatment may stalemate and/or be interrupted. The clinician must be courageous and intuitive but not foolhardy or aggressive. What a thin and difficult line to walk!

The clinician must be vigilant in avoiding using his/her life experience intuitively as does the mother. The patient is not the clinician's child and the patient's emotional history is quite different from the clinician's. The competent psychodynamic psychotherapist would have the ability to make these distinctions and be interested and accessible to small clues about the patient's emotional history without substituting his/her own history into the area of the *pre-verbal blur.*

Joanne is a good example of someone placed on meds who should not be on meds. The next case is the reverse.

Example 2

Alex was a twenty-year-old high-school dropout. He had been an excellent student in grammar and middle schools. But about the time of his sophomore year his grades began to slip. He managed to get through his sophomore and junior years because he was smart and knew how to work around some of the academic demands made on him. During his senior year, his performance was erratic, sometimes he did produce and other times he did nothing. The school warned that he might not graduate because he was not attending classes regularly and not turning in homework. The guidance counselor tried to help him get back on track. She knew he was above average in ability and had a good record until his last two years. She wondered how to help him. The counselor and many of his teachers were telling him he needed to put out more effort and to "get motivated."

His parents were puzzled at first and then became more and more angry. Alex was easily irritated whenever he was questioned about school, about the hours he spent on the computer, about the friends he was hanging around with, and about his increasing disrespect toward his parents. Tempers flared and the family was embroiled in emotional turmoil.

Finally, Alex's parents forced him to meet with them and a "therapist/counselor." Several weeks of work followed. Alex's problems were believed to be the result of family dynamics. Family history was explored, relationship conflicts reviewed, and efforts made to resolve the hostilities between Alex and family members. After three months with some small benefit, this therapy trailed off and ended.

In time, the family sought help from another therapist who took some family history and commented on some of the family dynamics and proposed to negotiate something of a "behavioral contract." The family and Alex were to agree on a few rules outlining their expectations and appropriate consequences regarding academic performance and respectful attitudes at home. Alex had a negative attitude toward the therapist after two sessions. The therapy ended shortly thereafter.

No one seemed to have an answer to Alex's increasing alienation from family and friends, increasing association with unsavory characters, increasing use of alcohol and marijuana, and increasing isolation. His parents made two more attempts to find help. As a last resort they arranged for a formal diagnostic battery of psychological measures on a recommendation from a friend who was a mental health professional.

The battery strongly suggested the presence of a major depressive disorder with ruminative anxiety and probable panic attacks. An evaluation for psychotropic medications was recommended. Alex and his parents returned to one of the previous therapists and brought the results of the psycho-diagnostic battery. The therapist read the report and felt that meds were not indicated and stated bluntly that he didn't believe in meds. He proposed an extended weekly treatment using cognitive/behavioral therapy (CBT). Three months later, Alex was arrested for driving under the influence.

The attorney representing Alex recommended another therapist. In desperation Alex and his parents tried once again. The therapist took a detailed family history and Alex's developmental history, noting the presence of depressive disorders in a number of biological relatives, the relatively quick, major change in Alex's mood, behavior, and academics, and his use of alcohol and marijuana. This therapist felt the psychological report was an accurate assessment of Alex's condition.

As a consequence of the diagnostic analysis, this therapist recommended that a trial of antidepressant medication be administered and monitored. During the next four months, a number of medications were tried and discarded. Finally a combination of Venlafaxine and Neurontin succeeded in returning Alex to his normal mood level and curtailing anxiety and panic attacks. No matter what a therapist's orientation, the notion that one treatment process is adequate to treat all patients is irresponsible. Given Alex's family history of depression, the relatively sudden onset of his symptoms, and the nature of the symptoms themselves all pointed to a more biologically induced mood state than an environmentally induced state. Alex and his parents agreed that the family was stable and secure. Friends thought "he had always had it made." Refusing to consider the possibility of an inherited vulnerability to depression and to exclude medications is a non-listening and irresponsible attitude. It is certainly not the way of a good psychodynamic psychotherapist.

IV

THE CHALLENGES OF THE CLINICAL EXPERIENCE

19

Countertransference and Rescue Fantasies

Whose regression is it anyway?

WHAT SHOULD BE THE RELATIONSHIP BETWEEN A PATIENT and a psychodynamic therapist? Should a therapist become a personal friend of a patient? Or a surrogate parent? Or a colleague? Or a business associate?

How does a therapist separate his "stuff" from the patient's? When is a therapist's "stuff" interfering with the therapeutic process? How is it that the same therapist treating similar patients will not necessarily have consistently positive results? No two patients are exactly alike, but that fact does not seem to completely account for the differences in clinical results. Small differences in similar patients hold clues to negative therapeutic reactions. Small differences account for the uniqueness of the specific interaction in the clinical situation. Melodies of mind are infinite in number and variety.

Countertransference is a complex, critical, clinical experience. It is an important therapeutic tool as well as a pitfall that may result in therapeutic failure. We will not review the extensive literature on countertransference. But we will try to identify the challenges and limitations a psychodynamic psychotherapist will face regarding the melodies of countertransference issues.

Countertransference, in its broadest sense, includes the therapist's social, psychological, political, moral, educational, and emotional reactions to patients. In its narrowest sense, it includes only those emotional reactions to patients which arise out of unconscious feelings derived from the therapist's early developmental years. Psychodynamic clinicians would agree that countertransference issues are derived from early childhood conflicts having to do with the total dependence and vulnerability of the child, the ambitions and need for mastery of the child, and the sensual and erotic needs of the child. Contemporary issues in a therapist's life can create countertransference also.

These derivatives may give rise to anxiety and/or depressive affects and may cause conflicts in the therapist. They persist throughout life. The conflicts never completely disappear. With healthy growth and development these conflicts are altered in the directions of adaptation, sublimation, and maturation. Every childhood derivative, every wish for satisfaction has to do with a particular person or persons, a particular set of memories and pleasures, all of which are unique for that child. And of course the child's significant objects and environment may be favorable or unfavorable in their effects on the child's mental life. So part of what constitutes the therapeutic relationship depends on the psychological state of mind the therapist brings to the relationship. The unremitting past may intrude itself in a disguised fashion into the therapeutic process with its own discordant melody.

A therapist needs to understand his or her own psychic development. Any patient may represent for the therapist a person of the past upon whom past feelings and wishes are projected. The patient reacts the same way to the therapist and the forthcoming transference moves the therapy forward. A therapist's conscious responses are usually thought to be countertransferential when they reach an inordinate intensity, or are strongly tainted by inappropriate sexual or aggressive feelings. Unconscious melodies of feeling arising from the vicissitudes of the therapist's development are largely responsible for countertransference.

Forms of Countertransference

There are several situations in the therapeutic interaction that may foster the emergence of unmanageable countertransference. For instance, one type of countertransference arises when the therapist identifies with the patient in the sense that the patient's unconscious fantasies and wishes match those of the therapist. Here it is important to distinguish between empathy and countertransference. In empathy the identification with the patient is transient. The identification with the patient is broken off at various times during the hour, allowing the therapist to internally reorganize his thoughts about the patient.

However, in an unmanageable countertransference, the identification continues and becomes caught up in conflicts identical to those of the patient. The therapist may act out or respond defensively. One person's empathy may be another person's countertransference. The classic "blind spot" is only one form of countertransference identification. In this case the therapist does not want the material from the patient to awaken his own memories and conflicts, so he misses making observations or interpretations that "connect the dots" for the patient. Or he may see the connections but not use this insight, again to avoid his own discomfort, and justify not making the interpretation by using various rationalizations.

The therapist could also divert the patient from continuing along the line where the therapist's unconscious material matches that of the patient's. For example, the therapist could offer an intervention that directs attention to other elements in the material offered by the patient so that the case stalemates. A psychodynamic therapist must have a readiness to recognize a melody from his/her own mind. We believe that a psychotherapist needs always to be on full alert when he is interacting more than usual with a given patient and ask, "What am I trying to help the patient and myself avoid by diverting and directing the particular session?"

Sometimes a therapist may take a moralistic stance and condemn in the patient what he cannot stand in himself. For instance, a patient's aggressive impulses may cause a therapist to become angry as it awakens the therapist's own aggressive impulses.

Another form of countertransference may arise from the nature of the material that the patient presents. These fantasies may be complementary rather than identical—such as the patient's wish to be rescued and the wish of the therapist to rescue. When certain patient fantasies are reworked by a therapist who has not gratified or sublimated longings to be a father, he may think to offer the grown-up patient a rescue in the form of insistence on his set of values. Or offer parental sympathy. This may well be the rationale behind some touching and soothing therapies as well as the unethical sexual misconduct of some therapists.

One form of countertransference disturbance arises from something in the therapeutic interaction that evokes the therapist's conflicts. Perhaps the therapist needs to show off his cleverness. Perhaps the therapist needs to have a competitive testing ground for competence and mastery. Here an early developmental framework is recognizable because these conflicts often arise in our juvenile years. For instance, a school situation brings back memories and conflicts concerning the wishes to excel, to master sports and academics. Or wishes may be hidden in the therapist's need to have the patient follow his/her advice or to engage the patient about the correctness of the therapist's interaction.

Again, all therapists face these forms of countertransference. A therapist who is trying to listen to the melody of the patient's mind must have a level of self-awareness sufficient to recognize, limit, and utilize his own melodies and manage the countertransference appropriately.

Patients vary in the level and intensity of their transference reactions to the therapist. The intensity of transference reactions from the "garden variety," "worried well," conflicted/symptomatic kinds of patients tends to be rather mild when compared with borderline or severely regressed patients. With the latter patient the therapist quickly experiences intense emotional reactions in response to the patient's premature, intense, and chaotic transference. In such cases, the therapist's capacity to withstand psychological stress and anxiety is the clinical challenge rather than with any specific problem of the therapist's past.

Thus countertransference becomes an important diagnostic tool that may define the patient's predominant emotional position in relation to the therapist. The more intense the therapist's emotional reaction to the patient, the more threatening it becomes to the therapist's neutrality. The more countertransference has a quickly changing and chaotic nature, the more likely it is that the therapist is in the presence of a severely regressed patient. So we emphasize again how important it is for a psychotherapist to listen to the melody of his/her own mind and be aware of his/her own unconscious conflicts in order to be clear about whose regression is it anyway!

Therapists want to feel good about what they do as much as people in other lines of work. One pitfall in psychotherapy is that the wish to feel good by doing good may not be therapeutic. Feeling good is an emotional state sometimes helpful in decreasing a professional's anxiety with a ready rationale. "If I feel good and the patient feels good then this must be the right thing called psychotherapy." Therapists who have conscious and/or unconscious "rescue fantasies," may feel good when they think they have saved the patient from a disastrous relationship.

The therapist, however, must be aware of the darker possibility. A disastrous relationship to the therapist may be a distorted report or may be important in non-verbal and non-behavioral ways. When the relationship is severed, the patient may become depressed and anxious. One of many pitfalls in the attempt to practice effective psychotherapy is that we can't predict consequences of our interventions.

Many relationships may be sustaining for a patient whether or not the patient feels good with it. If a sustaining relationship is fraught with difficulties and the patient is compliant and believes that he should do what the therapist suggests, then the patient may get worse and the treatment break off. We believe too many therapists proceed in this manner.

A stalemate may also occur. The therapist may have felt that she was rescuing the patient from a bad relationship. In a good therapeutic situation, the patient must develop the strength to assess the relationship and come to a decision regarding it in a more autonomous manner. The therapist learns to automatically examine his/her own psychology to prevent countertransference reactions to the patient.

A good example of a therapist trying to rescue a patient as a result of his own countertransference is seen in the case of Jay, who consulted a therapist because of an "impossible and demanding" wife. After listening to Jay's complaints regarding his wife and how she was "always angry" and critical of him, the therapist's unresolved conflicts with the women in his life were stimulated. He responded to Jay's complaints based on his own personal experience rather than with objectivity and clinical experience. He failed to do a thorough assessment of Jay's beliefs and attitudes, and assumed that he had a sufficient psychological grasp of Jay's wife. Therefore he felt, based on personal experiences rather than on the clinical material, that Jay should immediately leave the house and seek a divorce. The therapist's own discordant melody drowned out the patient's.

In spite of his complaints, Jay did not want a divorce. Jay became conflicted. The therapy stalemated. Jay sought a consultation with another therapist. After a few sessions, the new therapist recognized what the first therapist had missed due to countertransference.

Picking up on the little discrepancies in Jay's narrative and mindful of some of the choices in words that Jay used, the therapist proceeded to ask Jay to elaborate with more detail about the incidents and exchanges with his wife. It did not take very long for the therapist to recognize the way in which Jay tended to distort the meaning of his wife's comments or her intent. When the therapist offered observations and clarifications about what may have been going on between Jay and his wife, Jay immediately recognized their accuracy. He became more open to exploring his own tendency to distort. Ultimately, instead of ruling the wife out of the picture, the therapist referred them to marital therapy as well as individual therapy. Neither of these two people, in spite of their loudly professed wishes for divorce, really wanted one. They have now successfully resolved most of their issues and are relieved to be together.

Countertransference comes in many forms. For example, a patient may identify with the therapist so much that the therapist may feel flattered or nervous. When the patient starts emulating the therapist's style of dress so that the therapist finds herself shopping for clothing in cities other than those where she would usually shop, she may feel flattered, intruded upon, or caricatured. The therapist may want to feel neutral about the issue, but finds herself annoyed. The patient may have greater financial resources so her shawl or sweater may be nicer. In addition to being annoyed the therapist may feel envy. The solution may be wearing more of a uniform: black sweater, black pants and a gray blazer. She may hope that if her clothes are neutral her feelings will follow suit.

This may work. Then of course her other patients may notice that she changed her style of dress and wonder why. The therapist may compensate by staying with her personal style when attending social functions. This way a pitfall may be avoided. That is, the therapist may avoid falling into a competition with the patient by recognizing and containing her countertransference feelings.

Many male therapists get into competitive power struggles with male patients based on fame, fortune, or intellectual prowess. The psychodynamic psychotherapist will recognize the competition and do some internal reflective work or arrange for some supervision or personal treatment. This therapist will then be able to neutralize the driving force behind the competition. Intolerance for ambiguity may be masked by a competitive drive and an intellectualized defense may be masked by a rationalization for therapeutic clarification.

While supervising an inexperienced psychotherapist who is quite passive in her responses to an aggressive patient, a reversal of the tendency to intellectualize may occur. The therapist acts dumb so as not to confront the patient's aggression and avoids the patient's feared hostility. There is a delicate balance involved. On the one hand there can be a therapeutic clarification made possible by asking questions of the patient. On the other hand there may be an attempt to hide the fact that the therapist cannot tolerate ambiguity and so avoids asking a question that might help the patient hear the ominous tone of his own aggressive melody.

Sometimes questions can serve to diminish the therapist's anxiety or to show interest in the patient or to clarify motivation and confront aggression. On the other hand, when questions are intrusive, invade a sense of privacy, or are humiliating or tactless, therapeutic tact is lost and the therapeutic alliance is weakened.

The psychodynamic therapist will not need to change her technique to diminish her own anxiety. She will be able to find means outside of the psychotherapy session to lessen her feelings of discomfort with the patient. Consultation and/or supervision, either group or individual, can be useful. Non-treating therapists will not have the identical countertransference issues as the treating therapist and will be able to offer a more benign and salient perspective on the case. There are two people in the psychotherapy session and only one of them should be anxious. Anxiety in the therapist is regressive. Again, as we said earlier, practicing effective psychotherapy is harder than it seems.

20

Feelings

The Sound and the Fury

THE PSYCHODYNAMIC THERAPIST NEEDS A CONCEPTUAL ARMAMENTARIUM that includes a theory of emotion. The mind is a phenomenon of brain function and its complex interaction with the environment and subsequent developmental processes. The therapist's work is with the discordant melodies created by the interactions of thoughts, beliefs, and feelings.

Emotion and Reason, Mind and Brain

The first function of the nervous system (brain and spinal cord) is to monitor sensation that is to react to the impact of external stimulations, one of the first developments of primitive evolutionary organisms. Recognizing external stimulations and dangers is required for any organism to survive. As an example of nervous system monitoring, one can cite the "fight or flight" defensive reaction to danger arising from visual and auditory perceptions. This reaction includes the well-known changes in muscle chemistry and blood flow and increases in adrenalin directed by brain functions. The anxiety and/or panic created by this brain function enhances responses that increase the chance of survival. Humans are sometimes sandbagged by this flight or fight function that is designed to help. Our anxiety can sometimes be great enough to freeze us to death instead of free us to survive.

It appears that the variety of human emotions (affects) are in large part derived from bodily sensations. This is a complicated and still an avidly researched dimension of human psychology. However, with regard to emotion and the body, we cannot ignore the facts. Our brains are connected via the nervous system to all parts of our bodies, and no one really doubts how much our feelings connect with our physical sensations and reactions.

Consider the language we use to express our feelings. "I have a knot in my stomach." "I was so afraid my knees were shaking." "He was so mad he could have chewed nails." "He was so mad he saw red." "They were so happy they were jumping for joy." "He could feel the hair on the back of his head stand up." "She was so excited she could feel her heart beating." "I was so disgusted I felt like throwing up." "She was so agitated she couldn't think straight." "He makes my skin crawl." These are some references to human feelings of joy, anger, fear, sadness, and disgust found in all languages. We would even include guilt, shame, envy, and jealousy as reflecting the underlying connection between feelings and body states. Again, the melodies are infinite.

The more basic the feeling the more likely it will have noteworthy bodily correlates. There are, of course, more subtle variations of human emotion such as awe, excitement, euphoria, melancholy, panic, uneasiness. There also seems to be what we call "existential affects," that is vague feelings of existence—the dim sense of consciousness probably arising from the midbrain and brain stem. Consciousness, not self-awareness. Neuroscience research is showing self-awareness and sense-of-self have many associated feelings. It seems likely that humans were feeling, sentient beings before they were thinking beings. They reacted more quickly to events because of emotions than they might have, had they reacted based on reason. The anxiety generated toward the "fight or flight" reaction was a survival mechanism to avoid danger.

That feeling state is not an intellectual exercise. Spitting out bad tasting food to prevent taking in poisonous or spoiled nourishment was not done by careful analysis. Emotions were earlier developments in human evolution and more essential to survival than reason. Emotions inform us concerning the nature of things. The primitive aspect of emotion challenges the therapist and the psychotherapy. Raw emotions may be hard to understand and tolerate. Emotions can be ignored but they cannot be eliminated or suspended without consequences to the treatment process.

The Sound and the Fury of Affect

A psychotherapist listens to a story. The story may or may not make sense. The story has content, some facts, some mysteries, sometimes the beginning and an end and sometimes the story is full of "sound and fury." Without the sound and fury the story might be better told to a friend, a minister, or a relative. It is the melody of the sound and the fury that makes the story essential to the ears of a psychotherapist.

Sounds of affects (emotions) reverberate in our ears, minds, and imaginations. The human voice is a fascinating orchestra of a variety of emotions. Joy, pleasure, and pride are positive emotions. Our patients usually don't sound these emotions in the beginning of treatment. But if we listen we are more likely to hear the melodies underlying fear, anxiety, depression, guilt, and shame.

Envy and Jealousy

Do envy and jealousy sound different from one another? We think they do. There are notes of longing in the envious voice and a note of anger in a jealous voice. An envious voice is more likely to sound immature and whiny with a trace of admiration, perhaps. A jealous voice may be strident, immature, angry, and resentful. Envy is an emotion that may derive from a relationship with one person. Jealousy may derive from a triangular relationship involving two other people.

Patients often blend stories involving envy and jealousy. Therapists may not listen for the distinction between these melodies so they may lose an opportunity to track down a central psychological theme to its underlying roots. These roots may involve the nature of a relationship so it might be helpful to distinguish between envy and jealousy.

Shame, Guilt, and Envy

Two emotions that are not often carefully differentiated are shame and guilt. The melody of shame is quiet, almost inaudible, and not well modulated. By contrast, the melody of guilt may be loud, defensive, and wide ranging in its tonal qualities. Shame's voice is self-absorbed. The content of the story usually has but one character. Alternatively, guilt often involves an assessment of two people. The guilty patient is usually guilty in relation to another character beside himself.

Shame and envy are affect melodies that are hard to listen to for many hours because the music is very simple and involves only one person. The tendency is to keep looking for action in a story involving other people. Shame and envy are hard emotional melodies for the therapist to tolerate. Shame and envy often derive from an immature relationship with another person and may present a transference paradigm that the therapist might prefer to avoid.

For example, the patient may wish to be held while the therapist wants the patient to interact and be appreciative.

There is very little action to a story about shame. There may be only one or two clues in any sentence that reveals we are listening to a melody of shame. Shame makes us hide ourselves. Sometimes a patient will lie, cover up, or deliberately mislead. The patient may try to redirect the content of the therapy hour. A listening psychotherapist will take note of the patient's redirection and assess whether to confront the patient, that is, "I notice you just changed the subject" or to say nothing and store the shift away for later therapeutic work. Sometimes the therapist may feel bored and mentally wander away from the work. Boredom may be a covering used by the therapist to avoid recognizing her own angry melodies.

When a patient wants to manipulate the therapist, shame and envy may be the background emotions in the patient's character. An attempt to control another person may be a defensive operation to salve low self-esteem. Some patients believe that if they can control the therapist then they must be pretty smart. These patients will try to control the issues of time and money and, if there are administrative forms, then they will try to control what the therapist writes.

Our experience in this type of control is best exemplified in the area of diagnosis. A patient may be ashamed of a more severe diagnostic category and become hurt and angry if the diagnostic code is not benign. Since there is usually a lack of confidentiality in job situations for most people, we use the most benign coding possible.

Overpowering Affects

Overpowering affects are those feeling states that come up with unregulated, unmodified sex and aggression for which religion evolved to modify, and failed. So we are left to dissect how these affects work technically. The easiest affect to identify is anger or rage. Hostility may be subtle and embedded in a socially appropriate behavior and so harder to recognize. Anger is the hardest melody for the therapist to tolerate. When the melody of rage is expressed, a question of uncontrolled aggression both within and without the consultation setting must be assessed.

Often at the first rageful explosion and threat of harm, the therapist is frightened—not simply anxious, but frightened. If the patient is not well known to the therapist, the fright is a good indicator of a difficult patient. But if the patient and therapist have been working together for a period of time and the rage erupts within the consultation room, we would expect anxiety and not fright. If a therapist is frightened by a new patient, it might be a good idea to apologize to the patient for any inconvenience and tell him that "I don't think I'm the right person for you but I will be happy to give you other names and there will be no charge for the consultation." Sometimes the therapist may choose to analyze her own reactions so as to diminish the frightened feelings. Those feelings may become modulated with analysis, personal treatment, and supervision.

If a therapist has been working with someone for a period of time and knows by the history that he has a "bad temper," then the therapist should not be surprised at blowups in the office. One might say, "It's okay to scream but not to break anything in the office including the therapist." Then the therapist must ask, "How can we understand your rage?" The patient may not be able to stop screaming and shaking and cursing and shouting, but he usually will not cause any physical damage. The therapist may then be anxious but not frightened.

Some therapists respond to the raging patient with the overbearing statement that he must control himself, or the therapist won't be able to continue to work with him. This threat of abandonment is not therapeutic. Silence is not good but a threat of abandonment is worse. A good psychotherapist will be anxious but not frightened during a well-known patient's rage reaction and will have the patience and technical expertise to help the patient ameliorate his rage.

A female therapist had a colleague who was treating a well-known alcoholic who became physically aggressive during alcoholic binges. Once the alcoholic banged on the car window of one of the therapist's patients and frightened her. The therapist took this issue up with her colleague and suggested that the patient be transferred. The female therapist was frightened that this strong, rageful, alcoholic man would harm the small-framed female patient. She knew that the melodies of any rageful alcoholic or any addict for that matter, warn of danger in the way of music in movies.

Often a well-known patient's rage is psychologically driven and relates to the escaped wish to murder the person that is the object of the rage. Most experienced psychotherapists have seen jealousy incite such rages. In such cases, a calm demeanor and some concerned reality-based questions will help contain the rage in the consultation room. But both patient and therapist must bear the intolerable affect of rage for a relatively short time that feels interminable.

When a well-known patient is furious with the therapist over a perceived slight, the therapist may be anxious but we hope not frightened. We can hear the patient screaming, "You just don't care about me, you go home but I have no one." First of all the patient is correct. The therapist cares about her but not the way one cares for a member of one's family. Unconsciously and sometimes consciously the patient wants to be a member of the therapist's family so that the therapist will care for her in a family way. From the patient's point of view we can see why she is furious with the therapist. Nevertheless the therapist may be anxious but should not be frightened.

In general, the more primitive the affect, the harder it is to bear for both patient and therapist. Primitive affects usually are derived from early one-on-one childhood relationships or from a severe psychiatric disorder. Often these relationships have physical and emotional excitement or traumata attached to them. The patient has not been able to work through these relationships and the subsequent psychological hardships continually revisit the patient and the therapist as the work continues. With each revisit, hopefully both patient and therapist improve and these affects become ameliorated and moderated. Not always, but almost always, the patient has a better grip on the relationships, and the affects become more fully integrated and stabilized.

Melodies of Anxiety

A little anxiety can sharpen our senses and ready us for action. Too much anxiety is disruptive. It makes the melody of the unconscious difficult for the therapist to hear. Too much anxiety drowns out our thought processes and judgment. For pragmatic, clinical reasons, we categorize anxiety into five forms. A good therapist needs to have some sense of these different qualities or forms of anxiety. Of course these forms are not mutually exclusive. One can experience them in many combinations:

Reality-driven anxiety—an external, identifiable threat of harm
Self anxiety—threat of humiliation or personal deficiency
Loss of object–love anxiety—threat of loss of love of object
Loss of object anxiety—threat of object absence or destruction
Psychotic anxiety—fear of annihilation or disintegration

Reality-driven anxiety is the fear we feel when there is a danger to our physical well-being. This is the most easily understood form of anxiety. If the anxiety does not escalate to acute levels or to panic, we may be better prepared to avoid or turn the danger away. Panic on the other hand, can impair reasoning and leave us more vulnerable. Sometimes adults can experience panic anxiety even when there is no real danger. These attacks usually relate to early childhood threats of physical harm that are unconsciously displaced onto a current but non-threatening situation. One female executive had a panic attack overtake her as she began to address a group of trustees. She had noticed one sour-looking trustee who unconsciously reminded her of her psychotic, dangerous father and she became frozen with fear. Not knowing what was happening to her made the experience unbearable and she left the podium for the ladies room in the middle of her presentation. Later in a therapy session she realized what had so disrupted her, she breathed a sigh of relief and in a following session reported a totally different experience when she saw the same trustee at another meeting that week.

Self-related anxiety arises when there is a threat of humiliation. The most intense anxiety of this type is felt when we fear that others will think of us poorly, that we will be embarrassed or humiliated by how we are perceived. Many find this kind of anxiety excruciatingly painful. For some it is overwhelming to the point of despair. When such anxiety is co-morbid with a vulnerability to major depression, suicidal ideation and/or impulses are common. In other cases one only has to think of the embarrassment or humiliation that a person feels who has been fired for poor performance on the job or the feeling of a student who fails subjects in school that his peers passed or the intensely painful feeling of a teen who isn't asked to the prom.

Another self-related anxiety arises when our identity, our experience of ourselves and our place in the world is disrupted. We can think of the many men who retire from their careers and die shortly after. They are left anxious about how to think of themselves. (What do most men ask after they meet another man and exchange names—"what do you do?" "I'm retired" just doesn't help many men whose identity is bound to their work.) We can also think of the loss of identity that occurs sometimes when a marriage fails. People can become weak in the knees or empty in the pit of the stomach when they think of themselves as not married anymore because after awhile a marital state becomes part of our identities.

The third form of anxiety is the most commonly understood. Someone we need to love us will stop loving us. They don't call it the deadly silence for nothing. A child experiencing a mother's rejection by her deliberate silence will find that silence unbearable—like being dead. We can all recognize the anxiety we feel when anyone we love and need seems to withdraw affection or caring interest.

Good psychotherapists can recognize the fourth form of anxiety, the anxiety that arises when we fear threats of loss of the people to whom we are close. Death of a child, parent, wife, husband; separation; divorce; illness; all of these events can trigger anxiety states as the person anticipates the emotional pain of the physical loss of the actual object of attachment. Anyone who has witnessed the look of panic on the face of a two-year-old whose mother has slipped from view down an aisle in a supermarket knows what we mean. You can almost hear the screeching melody of fear.

Adults retain certain vulnerability to feelings of abandonment if once experienced as children. Just as the executive panicked at the sight of a trustee who looked and sounded like a feared parent, adults can experience acute anxiety and panic if they were raised by a parent or parents who neglected them or who threatened to leave, or did leave the child alone or was detached and emotionally unavailable. Many adults who have acute anxiety attacks as the result of pending separations or divorces are re-experiencing those childhood emotional traumas.

Finally, a psychodynamic therapist must be able to recognize the anxiety that accompanies the psychoses—schizophrenia, psychotic depression, and severe mood disorders. This kind of anxiety is most commonly seen in inpatient settings and hospital emergency rooms but does show up in outpatient settings more frequently today than in the past because of changes in the way health care is delivered. The patient is agitated and angry and paranoid as a result of psychotic anxiety driven by paranoid fantasies of personal annihilation. "I am being followed." "I must do 'blank' or I will be doomed." "I must go into the subway to be safe." We explored this form of anxiety in the spectrum disorders section.

21

Negative Therapeutic Reactions

"The unexpected always happens." "No it doesn't!"

THE NEGATIVE THERAPEUTIC REACTION is an intense dramatic shift in the treatment process that may result in a treatment disruption, suicide, homicide, or a shift into a severe regression and would not have been predicted from the previous psychiatric history or treatment. It is unexpected but contrary to the common folk wisdom, therapeutically it does not always happen. In fact, it is not a common event. A negative therapeutic reaction is a dramatic worsening of the patient's psychological behavior that cannot be accounted for by environmental influences such as physiological or neurological stress. A negative therapeutic reaction evolves out of misdiagnosis, mishandling of the transference, or a disruption of the boundaries of the psychotherapy situation.

Sometimes the patient's individual psychopathology is severe enough to drive a good therapy situation into a negative mode, worsen the patient's condition, and leave the therapist helpless. A moderate environmental or physiological stress might drive a therapy into the negative phase because the therapist is unable to alleviate the stress and the patient is unable to adapt to it. When a severely depressed person develops cardiac or neurological trouble, he may not be able to withstand the further assault on his ego. Although, interestingly enough, many psychiatric patients do quite well in adapting to the stresses of increasingly poor physical health. In such cases we usually do not see a negative therapeutic reaction if the treatment remains stable. Sometimes the patient may have access to medications that are potentially harmful if taken incorrectly and the patient may attempt and/or succeed at suicide.

The signs and symptoms of a negative therapeutic reaction may be sudden and intense and many of them may not occur in the consultation room. Increased destructive behavior either in the office or outside may show up as continuous suicide attempts, homicide, felony assaults, masochistic promiscuous behavior, illegal sexual behaviors, or dramatic and unforeseen emotional instability. Cognitive deterioration or physiological reactivity in a previously healthy person may indicate a negative therapeutic reaction.

The etiology may involve misdiagnoses, incorrect handling of the transference, poor technique, breaking confidence, boundary violations, and improper follow-up. If both the therapist and the patient feel helpless, hopeless, and lost, the foundation is laid for a negative therapeutic reaction.

Often we may hear of poor outcomes after the patient dies and we piece together the part that a negative therapeutic reaction played. These cases are analogous to doing a postmortem where the body doesn't give a good enough accounting of the cause of death. Suicide is a good example. Suicide among male adolescents on college campuses is a worrisome occurrence. John was a twenty-year-old sophomore who had high ambition and who was disappointing himself socially and academically. He had been evaluated for anxiety and depression and given antidepressants and a stimulant.

Follow-up appointments were scheduled for six weeks. He started his medication but discontinued the antidepressant. He decided to increase the dose of the stimulant and then in a sudden slough of despondency, took all the stimulant pills in the bottle. The only information the postmortem yielded was that he died of an overdose. Follow-up was improper. The patient was abandoned. The holding boundary of psychotherapy was promised and hoped for but not delivered. The patient died from his own psychopathology but had John been in ongoing weekly psychotherapy and the same outcome occurred, the suicide would be seen as a negative therapeutic reaction.

Jimmy was an eight-year-old boy who was referred for therapy because of school failure. He did not read, write, or interact with the other children in his class. His home life was troubled. Jimmy and the therapist began to play together on a weekly basis. The therapist did most of the talking. After awhile Jimmy picked up some of the toy cars and again got going. The therapist was happy. Jimmy began to make appropriate car comments. His language was fine. After a few months the school reported that he was doing his homework and was interested in the other children. This treatment was going well.

Suddenly, the therapist received a subpoena to appear in court. Jimmy's non-custodial parent was interested in custodial rights. The therapist did not want to break the confidence of the treatment situation and asked for a closed session with the judge and attorneys involved. The judge denied the request. The parent then told the child what was said in court and probably said a few hostile things about the therapist. Jimmy was brought to the office three more times but never played with the therapist again. He regressed to the time when he was non-interactive. He had a negative therapeutic reaction due to the sudden and dramatic breaking of the boundary of privacy.

Sara was a graduate student who was referred by a therapist who had been seeing her in intensive psychotherapy for about six months. He said that her cognition was developing a paranoid flavor and her physical health was deteriorating for no apparent reason. He was concerned that the transference was developing along psychotic lines. The second therapist agreed to see Sara and began a more supportive therapy without any therapeutic ambition but rather a waiting attitude. Sara felt relieved. As time went on, her physical health improved. Her paranoia quieted and her graduate studies picked up again. The first therapist recognized a negative therapeutic reaction and transferred the patient without abandoning her.

A less positive outcome occurred with Adele, who was referred to another therapist by a colleague for similar reasons as Sara. Adele was a failed college student who had been hospitalized on several occasions for assaultive behavior and depression. Adele was seen twice weekly in a psychodynamic, insight-oriented, interpretive psychotherapy designed to improve her ego functioning. But the therapist didn't pay enough attention to the reasons for Adele's hospitalization. Transference interpretations regarding her aggression did not occur to the therapist, who was young and inexperienced. The therapist could not understand why Adele would be angry with her, the therapist, when she was only trying to help. The near-psychotic proportions of the transference was underestimated. One day as the therapist left the office she noticed Adele's car in the parking lot. Later the therapist noticed Adele's car following her too closely. At that moment, the therapist realized that Adele had the capacity to use the car as a weapon and became quite frightened. She did not drive home but to the house of a friend who lived on a busy street. At the next appointment the therapist took up the issue of Adele's following her and the fact that she believed the therapist was harming her. Adele was then re-hospitalized. The therapist then made a referral to a different therapist. She interrupted the treatment because she recognized the negative therapeutic reaction. She believed the patient intended to harm her and felt unable to tolerate her own anxiety.

The risk of continued treatment in the face of a negative therapeutic reaction must be judged according to the possible benefits and outcome. Often the patient makes the judgment for us and we may speculate but never know. The unconscious melodies of these patients can be very scary to any therapist. Training and supervision are the only tools available to help manage this.

22

People Psychotherapy Probably Can't Help

The not-so-workable variations

The Sociopathic Spectrum

THE TALKING CURE CANNOT HELP EVERYONE. One major group of individuals who cannot be helped much are those who fit in what we shall call the extreme end of the sociopathic spectrum. Their melodies are rather alien to most humans. These are people who, to varying degrees, violate basic human values. A small percentage of the population, they are nevertheless a major disruption to any society and foster insecurity in any population. They may lie, cheat, steal, defraud, and in some cases commit acts of violence, including torture and murder, as a way of life. Their melodies of mind may be crude and heavy, smooth and sophisticated, ominously loud, or light and charming. The themes of the sociopath can also be quite sweet and seductive and the therapist needs to hear the hidden chords that warn of duplicitousness.

Such people may be found in all walks of life, from the common petty thief to the chairman of the board of a large corporation. The group includes business people, professionals, blue-collar and white-collar workers, old and young, men and women. Some may be violent, vicious murderers while others may have no violence in them at all, just a willingness to defraud. So the range is from mild to severe in seriousness and from crude to sophisticated in application.

The PDM understands such a personality as lying on a continuum from a socially active/manipulative "normal" style to a severe personality disorder such as the "malignant narcissist."

The DSM-IV-TR describes this "Antisocial Personality Disorder" as having a pervasive pattern of disregard for and violation of the rights of others. It indicates that this pattern has been present since age fifteen and includes a combination of three or more of the following behaviors:

- failure to respect the law and risking arrest
- being deceitful, lying, using aliases, conning others for personal gain
- being impulsive or not planning ahead
- being irritable and aggressive, including physical fights or assaults
- recklessly disregarding the safety of self or others
- irresponsible regarding work behavior or financial obligations
- lacking in remorse, being indifferent or rationalizing hurting others.[1]

Examples of antisocial personality disorder are plentiful in the movies for obvious dramatic reasons. A list of movies depicting this disorder would include, *A Few Good Men*, *Anatomy of a Murder*, *A Place in the Sun*, *A Clockwork Orange*, *In Cold Blood*, *The Postman Always Rings Twice*, *Dial M for Murder*, and *Wall Street*. There are many others, of course.

As we indicated in Part I, the DSM-IV-TR description has limitations. It is too narrow and offers no description of the inner world of sociopathically inclined individuals. The PDM does. People in the sociopathic spectrum are likely to vary significantly in their psychodynamics. Many, if not most, researchers and clinicians would agree that some, but not all, such personalities, often lack certain, important adaptive traits. Some clinicians think that sociopathic individuals feel no anxiety at times when most humans would. Other clinicians think that such individuals lack any sense of attachment, love, and/or loyalty. It is widely perceived by clinicians that many, but not all, of these individuals lack a well-developed conscience.

Patients manifesting sociopathic tendencies may have the potential to benefit from psychotherapy if they do have some vulnerability to anxiety plus some sense of attachment and loyalty in their history. Otherwise these patients are not candidates for psychotherapy.

Many explanations are offered regarding how such people come to be as they are and why they are not able to benefit from the talking cure. We simply wish to emphasize that the issue for therapists is the need to carefully evaluate such patients, (usually sent by the authorities or an attorney) to determine if the patient is one who cannot be helped or one of those who has some modicum of attachment and conscience, who might be helped.

Substance Abuse

There are people who are unlikely to benefit from therapy because they abuse substances sufficiently to become addicted or dependent. Heroin, cocaine, alcohol, and painkillers are not only addictive substances, but they also tend to make effective psychotherapy impossible because patients are not ready and able to engage in the therapy process. Their motives and perspectives are shaped by the need for the substances and not sufficiently by the need to resolve their problems. When the active adult recovers and has some interest in remaining free of substance abuse, psychotherapy may be an important adjunct for a drug-free life.

A rather dramatic example of this is seen in Max, a forty-three-year-old freelance heavy equipment operator, who sought the help of a therapist because he had been arrested for the third time in as many years for brawling in a bar. He reported a twenty-year history of cocaine and alcohol abuse. His concern was that the cocaine was beginning to affect his mental faculties. Sometimes after a cocaine episode he felt paranoid and "very weird and crazy." Brawls were becoming more common. His anxiety level was up. A cousin, who happened to be a physician, provided him with Xanax for his episodes of panic. "I need to get straight," he lamented.

Max talked a good game but one could discern, even as he referred himself to therapy, that his underlying wish was to find a way to limit his anxiety and his moments of "weird and crazy" without having to change his exciting, hyperactive way of life and give up the cocaine and alcohol. One more fact came to light during the evaluation. Max had a lifelong bipolar disorder. When the therapist presented this finding, Max responded, "Yeah, that's what the docs suspected eight years ago, But I've done okay. I just don't want to get crazy and burn out."

The therapist advised that Max's substance abuse constituted to a significant degree self-medication for the bipolar disorder. Max was told that clean and sober was the way to go. Then Max was told his bipolar disorder must be treated because attempts to quit cocaine and alcohol were doomed to failure without psychotropic medications. Max pushed back into the chair in dismay and exclaimed, "I don't want to take drugs." The therapist was hard-pressed to keep from laughing out loud. Max saw this and smiled a bit, "I know, I know. But I want to do this myself."

It is not hard to recognize this patient's wish to continue using cocaine and alcohol. He simply wanted to rid himself of the side effects they caused. Psychotherapy for Max wasn't about resolving inner conflicts or about containing his bipolar symptoms but about symptom management so as to continue his lifestyle with drugs.

Max was rearrested eight months later and sent to jail for "going crazy" on some guy in a barroom brawl. Even a great psychotherapist can't help when competing with the siren song of a major addiction.

Certain Personality Disorders

Other people for whom psychotherapy might not be helpful are those with certain personality disorders other than the antisocial personality disorder. The schizoid personality disorder is not often seen in clinical settings. The disorder is characterized by the DSM-IV-TR as "a pervasive pattern of detachment from social relationships in a restricted range of expression of emotions in interpersonal settings."[2] These individuals appear to have little interest in intimacy and are not likely to express feelings and experience pleasure. Friendships tend to be superficial. They choose to spend most of the time alone and do not engage in activities that include significant interaction with others. They can be caught up in a situation and become driven and obsessed on occasion. Examples of schizoid personalities can be found in books such as Albert Camus's *The Stranger* and movies such as *The English Patient* and *Remains of the Day*. Psychotherapy does not seem to work in these cases.

Many but not all narcissistic, schizotypal, histrionic, and paranoid personality disorders are also quite limited in their capacity to benefit from psychotherapy. Each patient of these types must be evaluated for suitability before proceeding with a dynamic psychotherapy effort. Some potential for forming a bond with the therapist must be present. The psychodynamic psychotherapist must be trained to assess whether the melodies of these minds can be rid of their discordant notes.

Notes

1. DSM-IV-TR, 701.
2. DSM-IV-TR, 710.

23

Rarely Encountered Disorders

> The difficult we do immediately; the impossible takes a little longer.
>
> —Motto: U.S. Army Corps of Engineers

SPEED-MINDED PSYCHOTHERAPISTS WOULD NOT DO WELL with the Army Corps of Engineers slogan. Unlike the slogan, psychotherapy is a difficult process and cannot be done quickly. Some psychological conditions are confusing with complicated melodies and will not improve even with the efforts of a therapist with a good ear. If a therapist practices long enough, he/she will be faced with an occasional patient who has an intractable disorder. Therapists need to be mindful that there are such cases, rare though they may be. We suggest that confidence must be tempered with humility. Training for a therapist should involve recognition of the patient who will be refractory to treatment.

What constitutes an intractable disorder? How do these patients differ from the people psychotherapy can't help as described in our chapter 22?

Let us answer the second question first. People with intractable disorders differ from people whom psychotherapy can't help because they possess certain, deeply embedded traits which frustrate any effort to explore their unconscious processes or to draw meaning from the work. People psychotherapy can't help may have personality disorders but do not have these particular traits. Or they may be seriously drug addicted, which is not a separate personality trait and with which therapy cannot compete. In addition, people who do not have these particular traits, even though they may have a serious psychiatric condition, are more likely to be successful in psychotherapy. The melodies of such people are often too discordant, too cacophonous, or have too many dissonant notes. We will offer some examples for the developing psychotherapist to consider.

An intractable disorder is one in which the patient's personality style or an Axis 1 (DSM-IV-TR) condition, whatever it might be, is complicated by certain ominous traits or behaviors. Michael Stone in his book *Abnormalities of Personality* suggests that the presence of certain traits predispose a person to be less amenable to successful psychotherapy.[1] Traits of special interest in this regard are sadism, sensation-seeking, vindictiveness, and perversion. The competent psychotherapist cannot be squeamish or unmindful of these traits and the effects they can have on the course of treatment.

Such traits can be the result of an underlying disorder or a separate aspect of the personality. The psychotherapist, after enough experience, will learn the difference. When the underlying disorder is something like a borderline personality, for example, it is possible and indeed often probable that sensation-seeking has developed in the patient as a means of escaping from intolerable emptiness typical of borderline conditions. On the other hand, sensation-seeking may be an integrated and ego-syntonic trait for a person who has defensively organized around avoidance and is challenged by the ordinary, unchanging day-to-day aspects of life.

Boredom sets in rather easily for sensation-seeking people. In milder or safer forms, the sensation-seeking person can take calculated risks and well thought out actions that are exciting without being foolishly dangerous or harmful to anyone. They may climb mountains, race cars, own motorcycles, travel more often, or become intensely involved in music, art, theater, and business ventures. In the more problematic forms, the person engages in more risky activity such as heavy social drinking, partying, drugs, multiple sex partners, gambling, and so on. When this dangerous behavior, is combined with a rather poorly integrated narcissistic personality or with someone in the bipolar spectrum such as a cyclothymic personality, the prospects for a successful treatment process are remote.

The same low probability for successful treatment is found in these types of narcissistic or cyclothymic personalities if sadism, vindictiveness, or perversion are embedded aspects of their mental status as well. For example, some people are imbued with strong sadistic trends in their personalities, and these trends so permeate the individual's experience of life that no amount of sifting through conflicts, cognitions, and affects will make any difference. Sadism comes in many forms and degrees. Sadism is not to be confused with what is commonly called passive-aggressive behavior nor should it be confused with vindictiveness. A sadistic person is enjoying the misery of another and takes pleasure in it for no reason other than the pleasure. Sadism can be part of a vindictive person's actions but there is at least a precipitating cause. Some clinicians consider sadism to be a perversion as in sadomasochism. The urge to tease, torment, or torture is quite driven by forces we do not understand well enough to influence the outcome of such a person's treatment in psychodynamic psychotherapy.

Vindictiveness is not all that uncommon or unusual. What we mean by vindictiveness as a trait is again, the extent to which it permeates a person's personality. The most famous public case of vindictiveness gone to extremes is a case of Barbara Broderick, the California woman who was so enraged at her ex-husband for divorcing her and remarrying a younger woman that she tormented them in a variety of ways and even drove her car into the front of the couple's house. In the end she broke into their house and shot them both dead. Her vindictiveness and need for vengeance was at the extreme end of the spectrum. To this day she has never indicated in any way that she regretted her actions. We think this is a clear manifestation of a malignant form of narcissism whereby the individual lacks the resilience to recover from a personal wound.

Perversions, now called perihelias, are another group of disorders that are, in general, not responsive to psychodynamic psychotherapy. With those perversions that seem to have been instigated later rather than earlier in the child's development, some success is possible. But most of the perversions, especially the hard-core ones (pedophilia, exhibitionism, fetishism), do not appear to have been successfully treated by any psychodynamic approach so far as we know.

Note

1. Michael Stone, *Abnormality of Personality* (New York: Norton, 1993), 423–53.

24
Non-Empirical Psychotherapists

Data is not the plural of anecdotal.

THERE ARE INNUMERABLE NOTIONS (alternative therapies) about how psychotherapy works in addition to the three more generally accepted models of insight-oriented, cognitive, and behavioral. Most of the other models are not grounded in reliable and valid empirical data and therefore rest wholly on the inclinations and biases of the individual "therapists" who practice them and very often on the idea that a sufficient infusion of love is needed. (Many of these therapists promote "hugs" as therapeutic.) The concepts supporting most of these models are bogus. They are based on anecdotal data and on unsupported notions of how therapy works. These "therapists" work with ideas they refuse to submit to scientific investigation and have their work reported only in journals that are not peer reviewed and are run by the "institutes" that promote their approach. Some of these therapists' operations are little more than cults. They insist either that conventional therapy is "just a theory" or that they are providing a valuable adjunct to the patient's efforts in psychotherapy or they are able to work with patients who are not treatable otherwise.

Physicist Robert Parks highlighted "seven indicators that a scientific claim lies well outside the bounds of rational scientific discourse." They can be summarized as follows:

1. The discoverer/practitioner pitches the claim directly to the media and the public, bypassing peer review and careful evaluation by others.

2. The discoverer says that powerful forces are trying to suppress his or her work. The idea is that powerful interests will try to stop or suppress their discoveries.
3. The scientific effect involved is always minimal or at the edge of measurement. For example, there is no clear photograph of a flying saucer, Bigfoot, or the Loch Ness monster.
4. The evidence is usually anecdotal. Modern science rightfully distrusts anecdotal evidence. Anecdotes are the way humans historically passed on information and have a very strong emotional impact. They serve to keep superstitious beliefs alive in an age of science. Anecdotes are not evidence.
5. The discoverer/practitioner says a belief is credible because it has endured for centuries. Myths persist that hundreds or even thousands of years ago, our ancestors possessed miraculous remedies that modern science cannot understand. Much of what is termed "alternative medicine" (as opposed to "alloplastic medicine," meaning "modern medicine") is part of that myth.
6. The discoverer/practioner has worked in isolation. It is hard to find examples of the lone genius who struggles against conventional methods and ends up making a revolutionary breakthrough in real life. Science proceeds through a synthesis of the work of many scientists.
7. The new "alternative" requires new laws of nature to explain it. The new law of nature, must not conflict with what is already known. If well established existing laws of nature must be changed to account for an observation, the alternative is almost certainly wrong.[1]

A few examples of alternative psychotherapies practiced by such psychotherapists and created out of the imagination of the "founders" without any hint of scientific evidence include "rebirthing," "past-life therapy," "neurolinguistic programming (NLP)," "co-counseling," "primal scream therapy," "applied kinesiology," "psychomotor patterning," "emotional freedom technique (EFT)," "regression therapy," "laying on of hands," and "thought field therapy (TFT)." There are many others.

It is unfortunate that these therapists are accepted within the popular culture as if they were practicing a valid form of treatment. Pseudoscientific, trendy, and quick-fix approaches to better mental health are understandably attractive to those seeking relief to their mental health problems. But imagine going to a therapist who attends to "human energy fields," or lays on hands to heal, or engages in a variety of rituals designed to "free the emotions." "Alternative" therapists are no more real alternatives to psychodynamic psychotherapists than homeopathic practitioners are alternatives to conventional physicians. Alternative therapies have been scientifically reviewed repeatedly and have been shown to be without foundation. Claiming that something that has been proven demonstrably false is still an alternative or a worthy competitor to valid scientific approaches (such as Intelligent Design as an alternative to Evolution) is essentially offering belief as evidence.

The example of Cassie in part one of this book is a case in point. This "therapist" decided that by hovering over a victim of sexual abuse and urging her to push him away, he could achieve a therapeutic effect. No supporting evidence or scientific rationale can be found for this nonsense anywhere.

"Rebirthing" therapy has gained adherents among anxious, despairing parents as a new, effective technique for the treatment of "reactive attachment disorder." Rebirthing is one of many alternative therapies that misappropriates Freudian concepts and uses pseudoscience to justify bizarre practices that capture the fancy of the unaware.

Practitioners of these unempirical alternative therapies try to gain legitimacy by peddling them as "complementary" to science-based treatments. When occasionally a clinician tries to be open to new ideas and goes along with an alternative therapy, it is then promoted as part of an "integrated" treatment. A number of university medical schools are flirting with such therapies to the consternation of most empirical scientists. These alternative therapies are almost all useless, can delay good treatment, and can sometimes be deadly. They are not even good examples of not-good-enough psychotherapy because they are not valid psychotherapies.

We cannot leave this topic without commenting on the pop psychology phenomenon. The self-help section of any bookstore has expanded dramatically in the past few decades. There are books aimed at helping people cope with every emotional struggle known to man—death and dying, depression, anxiety, narcissism, marriage, divorce, child rearing, opposition apathy, anger, attention deficit disorder, love, jealousy, and so on. Some of the books are well written by capable, knowledgeable people. But many more oversimplify, or offer formulaic fixes or New Age nostrums and how-to-feel-good philosophies.

Among the most dismaying pop psychology practitioners are those celebrity psychologists who are really entertainers. These are the "Dr. so-and-so's" who promote their commercial interests by practicing a kind of "public therapy" through blunt, dismissive, and demeaning attitudes as if it is helpful to browbeat, shame, and lecture. We feel strongly that these "doctors" are not doing anything helpful and may indeed be doing harm.

Note

1. Robert Park, "Seven Warning Signs of Bogus Science," *The Chronicle of Higher Education* (January 31, 2003).

Closing Comments

IN THE PRECEDING PAGES, WE HAVE TRIED TO HIGHLIGHT what we believe to be the most important aspects of our clinical experience as psychodynamic therapists. Where therapy and practice may be relevant to the character and development of the therapist, we have touched on clinical issues. Our hope is that this informal approach will allow the reader to take our perspectives into consideration free from the pressure of the academic viewpoint.

This book is about the psychodynamic therapist. Since the therapist works with patients, we have been obliged to elaborate the clinical setting in order to amplify the person of the therapist. The psychodynamic therapist must be broadly experienced and broad-minded to be effective in working with patients. Although common psychological conflicts and common defenses are found in most human beings, each has a unique organization of thoughts, behaviors, and feelings. Each patient has her own melody of mind, filled with both consonant and dissonant chords and notes.

A psychodynamic psychotherapist we have in mind has a spirit of adventure and a nonjudgmental willingness to listen and observe in novel ways within a complex set of constraints. She may have the gratification of sharing dramatic and subtle shifts in the patient's attitudes, emotional state, and behavior and the opportunity to develop a sense of fulfillment from a life's work.

Suggested Reading

This selection is a limited one and is intended to offer only some of the basic readings in the theory and practice of psychodynamic psychotherapy.

Theory of Mind

Arlow, Jacob. Unconscious fantasy and disturbances of conscious experience. *Psychoanalytic Quarterly* 38 (1969): 1–27.
Brenner, Charles. Conflict, compromise formation and structural theory. *Psychoanalytic Quarterly* 71 (2002): 397–417.
———. *The Mind in Conflict.* New York: International Universities Press, 1982.
Fonagy, Peter, Gvorgy Gergely, Eliot Jurist, and Mary Target. *Affect Regulation, Mentalization, and the Development of Self,* 1st ed.. New York: Other Press, 2005.
Fonagy, Peter, and Mary Target. Playing with reality I: Theory of mind and the normal development of psychic reality. *International Journal of Psychoanalysis* 77 (1996): 217–33.
Freud, Anna. *Adolescence. Psychoanalytic Study of the Child* 13 (1958): 255–78.
———. The Ego and the Mechanisms of Defense. *The Writings of Anna Freud,* vol. 11, New York: International Universities Press, 1936.
———. *Normality and Pathology in Childhood.* Penguin: Harmondsworth, 1965.
Freud, Sigmund. Fragment of an Analysis of a Case of Hysteria ("Dora"). *The Complete Psychological Works of Sigmund Freud—Standard Edition,* vol. 7, 3–122.
———. Inhibitions, Symptoms and Anxiety. *The Complete Psychological Works of Sigmund Freud—Standard Edition,* vol. 20 (1925), 87–124.

———. The Interpretation of Dreams. *The Complete Psychological Works of Sigmund Freud—Standard Edition,* vol. 5., (1900), 509–621.

———. Neuro-Psychoses of Defense. *The Complete Psychological Works of Sigmund Freud—Standard Edition,* vol. 3 (1894), 43–68.

———. The Psychopathology of Everyday Life, *The Complete Psychological Works of Sigmund Freud—Standard Edition,* vol. 6 (1901), Chapter 12, Determinism, 239–79.

———. Three Essays on the Theory of Sexuality. *The Complete Psychological Works of Sigmund Freud—Standard Edition,* vol. 7 (1905), 125–243.

Freud, Sigmund, and Josef Breuer. *Studies in Hysteria,* The Penguin Freud Library, vol. 3. New York: Penguin Books, 1991.

Hartmann, H. *Ego Psychology and the Problem of Adaptation.* New York: International Universities Press, 1958.

Jacobson, Edith. *Depression.* New York: International Universities Press, 1971.

———. The self and object world: Vicissitudes of their infantile cathexes and their influence on ideational and affective development. *Psychoanalytic Study of the Child,* ch. 9 (1954), 75–127.

Kernberg, Otto. *Internal World and External Reality: Object Relations Theory Applied.* New York: Jason Aronson, 1980.

Lear, Jonathan. *Open Minded: Working Out the Logic of the Soul.* Boston: Harvard University Press, 1998.

Mahler, M. S., F. Pine, and A. Bergman. *The Psychological Birth of the Human Infant.* New York: Basic Books, 1975.

Mayes, L. C., and D. J. Cohen. Children's developing theory of mind. *Journal of the American Psychoanalytic Association* 44 (1996); 117–42.

Moore, B. E., and B. R. Fine, eds. *Psychoanalytic Terms and Concepts.* New Haven, Conn.: Yale University Press, 1990.

Pine, Fred. *Drive, Ego, Object, and Self: A Synthesis for Clinical Work.* New York: Basic Books, 1990.

Schwartz, Andrew. Drives, affects, behavior and learning: Approaches to psychobiology of emotion and to an integration of psychoanalytic and neurobiologic thought. *Journal of the American Psychoanalytic Association* 35, part 2 (1987).

Spitz, R. A. The smiling response: A contribution to the genesis of social relations. *Genetic Psychology Monographs* 46(1946): 57–125.

Stern, Daniel. Affect in the context of the infant's lived experience: Some considerations. *International Journal of Psychoanalysis* 669 (1988): 233–38.

———. *The Interpersonal World of the Infant.* New York: Basic Books, 1985.

Swick, Helen, Mary Ladd Gawel, and Martha Perry Gobbon, eds. *The Collected Works of Harry Stack Sullivan,* vol. 1. New York: Norton, 1964.

Winnicott, D. W. The capacity to be alone. *International Journal of Psychoanalysis* 39 (1958): 416–20.

———. *The Maturational Processes and the Facilitating Environment.* London: Hogarth, 1963.

———. Transitional objects and transitional phenomena: A study of the first not-me possession. *UP* 34 (1953): 89–97.

Psychopathology

Alliance of Psychoanalytic Organizations. *Psychodynamic Diagnostic Manual: (PDM)*, 2006.

American Psychiatric Association. *Diagnostic and Statistical Manual of Mental Disorders DSM-IV-TR Fourth Edition (Text Revision)*, 2000.

Ben Bursten. *The Manipulator: A Psychoanalytic View*. New Haven, Conn.: Yale University Press, 1973.

Deustch, Helene. Some forms of emotional disturbance and their relationship to schizophrenia. *Psychoanalytic Quarterly 11* (1942).

Erikson, Erik. *Way of Looking at Things: Selected Papers*. W. W. Norton & Company, 1996.

Faris, Gerald A., and Ralph M. Faris. *Living in the Dead Zone: Janis Joplin and Jim Morrison: Understanding Borderline Personality Disorders*. Ashland, Ohio: Slade Books, 2001.

Green, Hannah. *I Never Promised You a Rose Garden*. Signet; 39th Printing edition, 1964.

Kernberg, Otto. *Borderline Conditions and Pathological Narcissism*. New York: Jason Aronson, 1975.

Khan, Masud. Clinical aspects of the schizoid personality: Affects and technique. *International Journal of Psycho-Analysis* 41 (1960): 430–37.

Kohut, H. *The Analysis of the Self. Psychoanalytic Study of the Child, Monograph #4*. New York: International University Press, 1971.

Krystal, H. Trauma and affects. *Psychanalytic Study of the Child* 33 (1975): 81–116.

McWilliams, Nancy. *Psychoanalytic Case Formulation*, New York: The Guilford Press, Inc., 1999.

Rako, Susan, and Harvey Mazer, eds., and Elvin V. Semrad (Author). *Semrad : The Heart of a Therapist*. New York: Jason Aronson, 1984.

Stone, Michael. *Abnormality of Personality*. New York: W. W. Norton, 1993.

Wälder, Robert. The Principle of Multiple Function: Observations on Over-Determination. *Psychoanalytic Quarterly* (1936).

Westen, D., and G. O. Gabbard. Developments in cognitive neurosciences:1. Conflict, compromise and connectionism. *Journal of the American Psychoanalytic Association* 50 (2002): 53–98.

Winnicott, Donald W. Ego distortion in terms of true and false self. In *The Maturational Processes and the Facilitating Environment* (140–52). London: Hogarth and the Institute for Psycho-Analysis, 1965.

Treatment

Allen, Jon G., and Peter Fonagy and Anthony Bateman. *Mentalizing in Clinical Practice*. Washington, D.C., American Psychiatric Publishing, 1st edition, 2008.

Arlow, Jacob. Unconscious fantasy. In *Psychoanalysis: The Major Concepts*, edited by B. F. Moore and B. R. Fine (155–62). New Haven, Conn.: Yale University Press, 1995.

Bender E: Gabbard explains dos and don'ts of teaching psycho therapy. *Psychiatry News*, April 15 (2005), 30.

Bion, Wilfred. *Experience in Groups*. New York: Basic Books, 1961.

Blatt, Sidney. Analytic understanding of depression. *Journal of the American Psychoanalytic Association* 46 (1998): 732–52.

Blos, Peter. *On Adolescence*. New York: The Free Press, 1962.

Blum, H. The conceptual development of regression. *Psychoanalytic Study of the Child* 49 (1994): 60–76.

Busch, Fred. *Rethinking Clinical Technique*. Aronson (1998).

Caligor, Eve, Otto Kernberg, and John F. Clarkin. *Handbook of Dynamic Psychotherapy for Higher Level Personality Pathology*. Washington, D.C.: American Psychiatric Publishing, 1st edition, 2007.

Freud, S. Remembering, repeating, and working through. *The Complete Psychological Works of Sigmund Freud—Standard Edition*, vol. 12, 1914, 145–56.

Fromm-Reichman, Frieda. *Principles of Intensive Psychotherapy*. University of Chicago Press, 1960.

Gunderson, John. *Borderline Personality Disorder: A Clinical Guide*. Washington, D.C.: American Psychiatric Publishing, Inc., 2nd edition, 2008.

Kantrowitz, J. L., A. L. Katz, and F. Paolitto. Followup of psychoanalysis five to ten years after termination: I. Stability of change, II. Development of the self analytic function, III. The relation between the resolution of the transference and the patient-analyst match. *Journal of the American Psychoanalytic Association* 38 (1990): 471–96; 637–54; 665–78.

Kernberg, Otto. Supportive psychotherapy with borderline conditions. In *Problems in Psychiatry* (180–202), edited by J. O. Cavenar and H. K. Brodie. Philadelphia: Lippincott, 1982.

Levy, S. *Principles of Interpretation: Mastering Clear and Concise Interpretations in Psychotherapy*. New York: Jason Aronson, 1996.

McWilliams, N. *Psychoanalytic Psychotherapy*. New York: Guilford Press, 2004.

Schafer, Roy. *The Analytic Attitude*. New York: Basic Books, 1983.

———. *A New Language for Psychoanalysis*. New Haven, Conn.: Yale University Press, 1976.

———. Talking to patients in psychotherapy. *Bull Menninger Clinic* 38 (1974): 503–15.

Searles, Harold. *Collected Papers on Schizophrenia and Related Subjects*. New York: International Universities Press, 1965.

Steiner, J. Psychic *Retreats: Pathological Organizations in Psychotic, Neurotic and Borderline Patients*. London: Routledge, 1993.

Stone, Leo. The widening scope of indications for psychoanalysis. *Journal of the American Psychoanalytic Association* 2 (1954).

Sullivan, Harry Stack. *Schizophrenia as a Human Process*. New York: Norton, 1962.

Tyson, Phyllis, "Sexuality, Femininity, and Contemporary Psychoanalysis." *Journal of the American Psychoanalytic Association* 78, Part 2, 385–89, April (1997).

Psychodynamic Psychology and Modern Science

Bertanlanffy, L. von. The theory of open systems in physics and psychology. *Science, III* (1964): 23–29.

Busch, Fred. (Ed.) *Mentalization: Theoretical Considerations, Research Findings, and Clinical Implications* (Psychoanalytic Inquiry Book Series). New York: Analytic Press, 1st edition, 2008.

Greenberg, R., Katz, Schwartz and Pearlman. A research based reconsideration of the psychoanalytic theory of dreaming. *Journal of the American Psychoanalytic Association* 40, 2 (1992): 531–50.

Main, M. Discourse, prediction, and recent studies in attachment: Implications for psychoanalysis. *Journal of the American Psychoanalytic Association* 41 (1993): 209–44.

Olds, David, and Arnold Cooper. Dialogue with other sciences. *International Journal of Psychoanalysis* 78, Part 2 (April 1997): 219–23.

Westen, D., and G. O. Gabbard. Developments in Cognitive Neuroscience: I. Conflict, Compromise, and Connectionism. *Journal of the American Psychoanalytic Association* 50, no. 1 (2002): 53–98.

Westen, D. The scientific status of unconscious processes: Is Freud really dead? *Journal of the American Psychoanalytic Association* 47 (1999): 1061–1106.

Other Readings

Churchill, Winston. *The Grand Alliance, Volume III.* Boston: Mariner Books (1986).

Paine, Thomas. *Common Sense.* Boston: Courier Dover Publications, (1997).

Park, Robert. Seven warning signs of bogus science. *The Chronicle of Higher Education,* January 31, 2003.

Sprengnether, Madelon. *Crying at the Movies: A Film Memoir.* Minneapolis, Minn.: Graywolf Press, 2001.

Trilling, Lionel. Freud and Literature. In *The Liberal Imagination.* New York: Doubleday, 1953.

Index

About the Authors

Rima Brauer, M.D., completed her training in adult psychiatry at the Yale School of Medicine and continued further training in child psychiatry at the Yale Child Study Center. She became a consultant in pediatric psychiatry for the Yale Department of Pediatrics and later for the State of Connecticut. A graduate of the Western New England Institute for Psychoanalysis in New Haven, she maintains a private practice in psychoanalysis and psychotherapy in West Hartford. She also volunteers as teacher and superviser of psychiatric residents at the Institute of Living and the Department of Psychiatry in the School of Medicine at University of Connecticut. Her work with patients, clinical teaching, and scholarship are informed by her deep commitment as a physician. In her spare time she cooks, plays with her grandchildren, and listens to her husband practice the violin.

Gerald Faris, Ph.D., is a clinical psychologist currently in private practice in Glastonbury, Connecticut. Dr. Faris has more than thirty years of hospital, private practice, and research experience. He directed clinical research and supervised interns for the adolescent inpatient psychiatric unit at Mt. Sinai Hospital in Hartford, Connecticut. He also supervised intern diagnostic evaluations at the Yale University School of Medicine where he was an associate clinical professor of psychiatry. Coauthor with his brother Ralph of *Living in the Dead Zone: Janis Joplin and Jim Morrison—Understanding Borderline Personality Disorder*, Dr. Faris is a veteran consultant for mental health facilities throughout the state of Connecticut and has lectured for many years on longitudinal research in schizophrenia, psychodynamic therapy, personality and mood disorders. In his previous life, he was a licensed professional mechanical engineer in practice for fifteen years before becoming a clinical psychologist.

www.ingramcontent.com/pod-product-compliance
Ingram Content Group UK Ltd.
Pitfield, Milton Keynes, MK11 3LW, UK
UKHW041937031026
476234UK00001B/6

9 780765 706133